Teruyuki Okazaki

In His Own Words

BY
JOSE M. FRAGUAS

LOS ANGELES, CA (USA)

DISCLAIMER: Please note that the author and publisher of this book are NOT RESPONSIBLE in any manner whatsoever for any injury that may result from practicing the techniques and/or following the instructions given within. Since the physical activities described herein may be too strenuous in nature for some readers to engage in safely, it is essential that a physician be consulted prior to training.

First published in 2018 by Empire Books/AWP.

Cover photo courtesy of Bill Bly.

COPYRIGHT © 2018 BY EMPIRE BOOKS/AWP LLC. All rights reserved. No part of this publication may be reproduced or utilized in any form or by any means, electronic or mechanical, including photocopying, recording, or by any information storage and retrieval system, without prior written permission from Empire Books/AWP LLC.

Library of Congress Catalog Number: ISBN-13: 978-1-949753-04-2

Empire Books/AWP LLC
P.O. Box 401788
Los Angeles, CA 90049

LIBRARY OF CONGRESS CATALOGING-IN-PUBLICATION DATA:
NAMES: Okazaki, Teruyuki, 1931- interviewee. | Fraguas, Jose M., interviewer.
TITLE: Teruyuki Okazaki : in his own words / [interviewed] by Jose M. Fraguas.
DESCRIPTION: First edition. | Los Angeles : Empire Books, 2018.
IDENTIFIERS: LCCN 2018042811 | ISBN 9781949753042 (pbk.).
SUBJECTS: LCSH: Okazaki, Teruyuki, 1931 -- Interviews. | Martial Artists -- Japan -- Interviews. | Karate -- Japan.
CLASSIFICATION: LCC GV1113.O53 A5 2018 | DDC 796.8092 [B] --dc23
LC record available at https://lccn.loc.gov/2018042811

TERUYUKI OKAZAKI

Foreword

I SPEAK NOT ONLY FOR MYSELF, but for all of the students who had the opportunity to train under Shihan Okazaki. How fortunate we were to have him as our teacher.

I always felt a great sense of anticipation prior to taking his classes at Honbu Dojo. As a young man just starting out in martial arts myself, I had deep respect for Shihan Okazaki's legendary abilities. Knowing Shihan Okazaki was a direct student of Master Funakoshi, and Master Nakayama. I was eager to learn all that he had to teach me.

His classes could have been perceived as deceptively simple. During class he taught many of the same combinations for years, always stressing natural body movement, and correct form. There were times during class he would burst out loud, his voice a deep growl, pushing us to train even harder. Then just as suddenly, he'd returned to the calm almost jovial state as before. I felt moments like those, in my gut.

The particular challenge of repetitive training, requires not just physical strength, but strong mental fortitude. It is this forging of spirit, that I developed and learned from his teachings. Simply stated this is what made him a great teacher.

HIROYOSHI OKAZAKI

TERUYUKI OKAZAKI

Acknowledgements

A BOOK OF THIS KIND cannot be written without the generous support of friends and colleagues, and I am indebted to all of them for their help to make this one possible. The importance of their contributions to the work cannot be overstated.

First of all, I would like to thank Teruyuki Okazaki Sensei who opened the doors, not only of his dojo, but also of his privacy and heart to me.

A very special thank you goes to Hiroyoshi Okazaki Sensei, who read an early version of the manuscript, shared his boundless passion for the project with me in many conversations, and furnished many of the photographs that appear in the book.

IN HIS OWN WORDS

To Lois Luzi, personal secretary to Okazaki Sensei, for all her help and encouragement with this project and throughout the years. She generously shared her extensive knowledge about Okazaki Sensei's life in many lengthy conversations. She carefully and patiently saw the project through to completion.

This book is a tribute to Okazaki Sensei and will shed more light on the man and his history but the intent is not to be a definitive work either on his life or on his many contributions to the art of karate-do.

Sensei always says that "life is about its events." It certainly is about its challenges, about our successes and failures, but above everything, it is about the people we meet; how we touch others and how we are touched by them.

It is my sincere hope that comes through in the pages of this book.

JOSE M. FRAGUAS

TERUYUKI OKAZAKI

INTRODUCTION

MANY TIMES OVER THE YEARS, I have listened to masters tell their experiences in the art of karate-do; about their childhood, about their struggles and the relations amongst the kohai and sempai, amongst the teachers and the sensei, etc. Often they would conclude by saying that they would like, someday, to write their autobiography.

IN HIS OWN WORDS

History is history because of the human activity and it cannot be accurately recorded unless it is looked at from the standpoint of the individuals who make it. In this work, we'll try to discover one man who played an extremely important role in the development of the Shotokan karate around the world.

The particular value of anything, or any person, must alter according to the time and place from which we take our view. That is why when Okazaki Sensei proposed to me to write this biographical work, I was caught by surprise —- he had just parted ways with the "Japan Karate Association". We were working on another book but he insisted that he wanted this one to be done before. After his retirement in 2015, this "idea" became more pressing for him, and he decided that it was the right time to start writing his story down.

Teruyuki Okazaki remains an icon of charming and effective leadership in the world of karate. He is a man of his own time – his own history – and a mentor for many of us. Although relatively inexperienced when he was sent by Nakayama Sensei to spread the art in the United States of America, the young Okazaki gave the impression that he was born with the skills that took him to be one of the most charismatic and powerful karate masters in the world.

To accomplish the task at hand, I began "secretly" to travel to Philadelphia for periods of seven to ten days to video tape and record hundreds of stories about his life to later on start putting them into written form. During the past few years, we have polished those stories, moved back into his childhood, forward into the early days of his training after the war, the creation of the "International Shotokan Karate Federation", into the times of his arrival to the U.S. and finally on the separation of the "Japan Karate Association" and his plans for the future.

He wanted to preserve some things that were said a long time ago, of which not many people today are aware.

IN HIS OWN WORDS

If you read carefully, you'll realize that Okazaki Sensei was not trying to become a "fighting machine" or simply training in order to be a fighter. He focused, rather, on how to use karate-do to become a better human being. "There are many links that, once discovered," he said, "open a wide spectrum of possibilities, not only to martial arts, but to a better existence as individuals. Karate-do is about the meaning of life."

Our interviews often lasted as long as three or four hours of non-stop talking. We would begin at the school in Philadelphia and finish the conversation at a restaurant or coffee shop. A lot of information had been never published before and some had to be trimmed, either at Okazaki Sensei's request or edited to avoid creating senseless misunderstandings.

The result is a very personal story. A young man who dedicated his whole life to one unique vision. It is the story of one man's life and ambition: to spread around the world the teachings and philosophies of his teachers: Grand Master Funakoshi and Nakayama Shihan.

This book is about the family and the childhood that shaped his dreams, about the karate experiences that sharpened his impeccable technique, and about the struggle to polish them to perfection. It is the story of an honest man who appreciated having choices. His rebellious nature gave him the courage to face down any obstacle and resistance successfully.

As a young man, he created his own structure when the existing one proved too unwieldy, surrounding himself with talented people, and learning what he needed to know to make solid decisions. He benefited from both his mistakes and his successes; and he was willing to put in the time and effort that each task required to accomplish his goal. None of these tenets were new, but they still have the power to provoke thought in potential leaders, not only karate leaders but leaders for a better world. Some elements of leadership were crucial in the development of ISKF: clear vision, avoid the status quo, resilience, charisma, communication, constant learning, team building, decision making, and crisis management. All these concepts were used by Okazaki Sensei in building one of the biggest organizations in the history of karate. Much of the Teruyuki Okazaki persona was carefully cultivated, and that today's karate leaders can also acquire these impeccable qualities. Nakayama Shihan was known to have said that Teruyuki Okazaki was rare in the karate world because he had the awesome skills of an excellent karate technician, and a critical mind for detail and organization.

    I have relied primarily on Okazaki Sensei's memory. But I have made use, however, of all the other help I could find; from long-time friends and family members that kindly went back to his family in Japan to gather information and photos that would make this book a unique work. I am extremely grateful for their help.

We have told the story as Okazaki Sensei lived it, as he heard it, as he understood it and as he told it to me. A few of the incidents I tell about some of those involved might rather forget. We hope they will forgive us. What we have told we have told because it is part of the story of who Teruyuki Okazaki is, how he thought, and how he felt during his years of spreading Funakoshi and Nakayama Sensei's legacies.

For my own part, I hope that this work will help the karate practitioners around the world understand a little better the person and story of a "heart full of fire".

The last "recording" session with this exceptional teacher took place at the ISKF main dojo in Philadelphia. Early in the morning he broke the routine, instead of waiting for his secretary to bring him the morning tea, he stood up, grabbed a cup that had been just prepared and then gave it to me. Then, he took one for himself and said: "Let's go outside." After bowing, we enter and crossed the dojo from the office door to the main door in the street. It was a very cold Philly morning. No jacket, no coat. He took a deep breath in, peacefully smiled while looking up and down the street that had been his "karate home" for more than five decades, like reminiscences of his own history were flashing back in his mind. He suddenly said: "we did it!," raised his cup of tea and started to talk about the meaning of life. He was talking from experience. I listened.

The teaching goes on.

JOSE M. FRAGUAS

Teruyuki Okazaki
In His Own Words

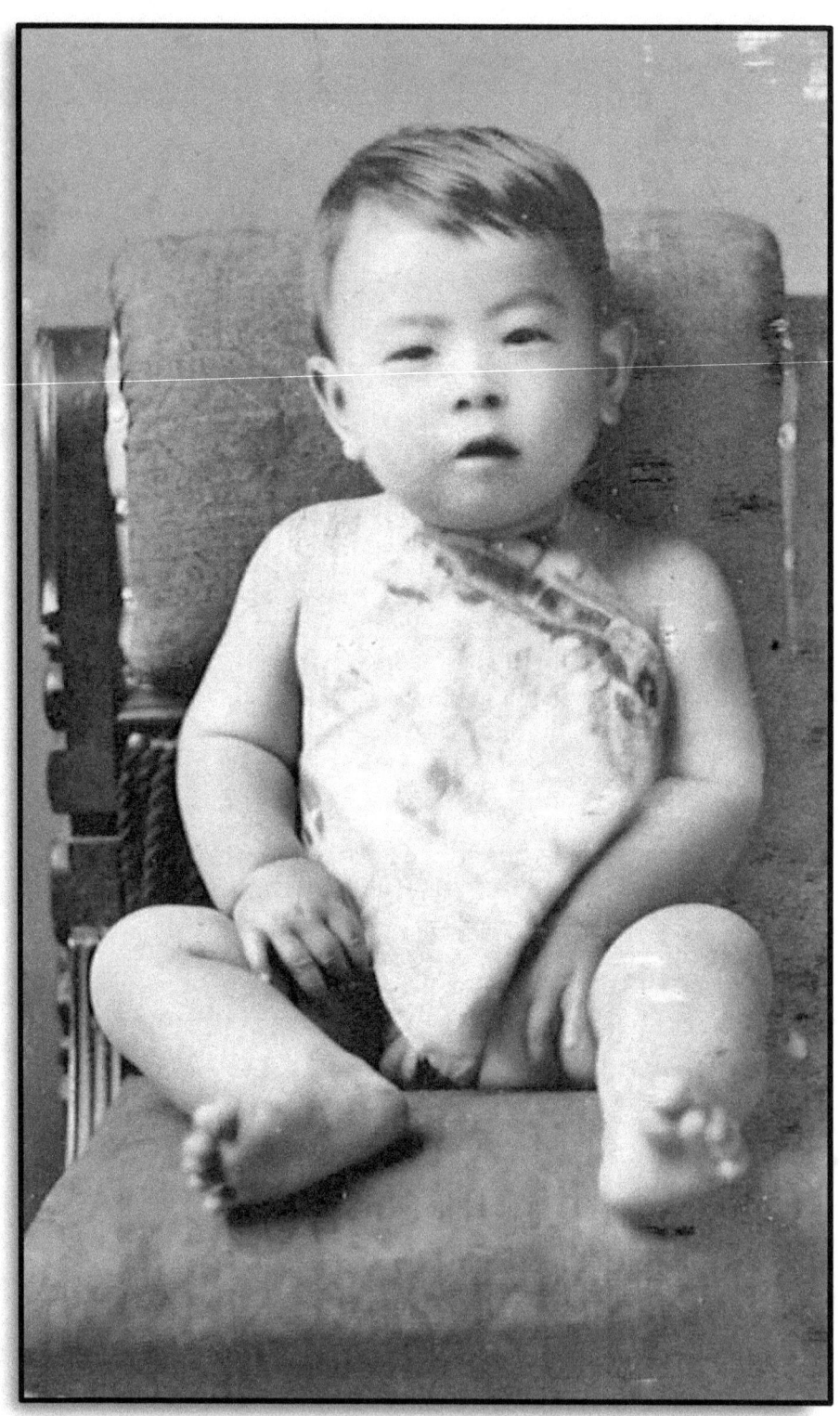

Teruyuki Okazaki at one year old

TERUYUKI OKAZAKI

In His Own Words

QUESTION: *Sensei, how was your childhood and early years with your family?*

OKAZAKI: It was a very traditional home. It is important to remember that one of the most important things in Japanese families after the war was for the children not to do anything that could embarrass the parents. You grow up making sure that anything of what you do will not bring any bad to your family. Unfortunately, I don't see kids being taught that way these days. For us, it was a very important thing. It is interesting to note that for my generation if a young man left his home with some kind of aspiration, there was no chance for him to return without having fulfilled it. For me it was karate. I'm not sure if I did accomplish much or not but I believe that I perpetuated the teaching from Funakoshi Sensei and Nakayama Sensei.

IN HIS OWN WORDS

*QUESTION: **How were your days as a young man?***

OKAZAKI: When you are a teenager is when you start moderating your character and personality. If the influences during those days are not correct, that will affect who you'll become. Human beings grow into adulthood using their innate life force and the knowledge coming from outside influences. It is important to have someone to look up to and a clear direction in life. Mine was karate-do. My best and worst things in life came from karate. It was my choice and I did stick to it. I have no regrets how I spent my youth. I had something that I loved with all my being. I see too many young people today not knowing what they want in life, and simply giving themselves to the satisfaction of whatever comes to them in the moment. An individual without aspirations is like a ship without a rudder. Unfortunately, there are many such people in our society.

QUESTION: Did you ever do any other kind of work besides teaching karate?

OKAZAKI: Yes, in Japan I had a restaurant. I could not cook but I ran the business. However, it took too much time from my training, teaching and coaching so I got out of that business.

QUESTION: Sensei, what do you think is the best age for training in karate?

OKAZAKI: There is no best age. Each phase of life brings different challenges and abilities. For the children, it teaches discipline and hard work as well as self-confidence. For the teenagers and college age students, of course they first think of sport karate. Then they begin to realize there is much more to be gained along with the hard work comes the patience to attain their goals. It's not like computers where all of the information is at the click of a button. Karate do takes hard work to be successful. The young people are our future and it is important to teach them the correct way and not to forget to include the Dojo Kun and Shoto Niju Kun. And for the older person we learn there is no end. Just like Grand Master Funakoshi trained until he passed away, so can everyone. As I said earlier, it takes a lifetime to learn karate and if we train smart we can always learn more from Heian Shodan and all of the kata. Also, for the older person, they understand the responsibility that comes with years of training which is to pass it on and be as much help as possible to guide the younger ones.

QUESTION: *Prior to studying Karate, you practiced Aikido, Judo and Kendo. Why did you never follow these as Martial Arts, and why did Karate become your chosen long-term commitment?*

OKAZAKI: I began training in Karate when I was a student at Takushoku University. There was something about it that I knew it was for me. It was very challenging and I knew it would take my entire lifetime to learn it. Of course being a

Teruyuki Okazaki's Parents' (Aikichi and Tsuneko) Wedding Photo

young person, there were times when I may have been impatient, but my teachers Master Funakoshi and Master Nakayama guided me, and after some time I began to help teach. I gave them my word that I would continue to practice and teach Shotokan Karate, always following Master Funakoshi's guidelines in the Shoto Niju Kun and Dojo Kun.

QUESTION: *Can you tell us a little bit about your family? Was everyone involved in martial arts?*

OKAZAKI: My father was a direct descendent from Samurai so his martial art training was in sword fighting. My brother who is older than I also trains in Shotokan karate and still does to this day. My sister was the youngest and studied martial arts in school because it was required of everyone.

QUESTION: *What was it like in school for you?*

OKAZAKI: I was a very bad kid. I was considered one of the tallest kids and because of this I was always in the back of the line. When I would be feeling mischievous, I would tease the other kids and push them. The teachers would tell my parents but my Grandmother always came to my defense. I think I was her favorite. (he says with a grin). My Grandmother had a very good insight into human nature. Everyone thought she was psychic. She also loved nature and would speak to the birds. She said you can learn a lot just from listening to nature and to never go against nature. When it was time for graduation from high school, the school told me I did not have to go to the ceremony. I was happy about this because I really didn't want to go anyway and I felt like I was special because of this. They said even if I was not there, I would still graduate and get my diploma. But in reality, they just didn't want me causing any trouble at the graduation. When I went home with the note from school saying I did not have to go to the graduation, my parents and Grandmother were very upset. They did not like that at all, so my Mother and Grandmother went to the school and insisted I be included in the graduation ceremony. The school had to agree and they let me go. And of course I did my best to behave. And my family were happy.

QUESTION: *You grew up during the time of the war, how did that effect you?*

OKAZAKI: Of course we were always taught our country was the best and we would never lose the Second World War. I think this is true for all countries. It teaches loyalty to your country and culture. Most young teenagers were taught that it was an honor to fight for your country and we did as was expected. When my time came to train as a kamikaze pilot my Mother was so sad. I told her not to worry, that I would be ok and it was the right thing to do. We were taught how to fly the plane but not how to land so we accepted that. Just as I was to start my flying lessons to be in the military the war ended. But when we were told the war was ending my friends and I did not believe it. We were still going to fight for our country. We left our homes and went and hid in a cave. We were going to wait there until the enemy came and fight them off. We didn't have any weapons but being young kids we didn't think that far ahead. We waited and waited and one of my friends said "maybe they are telling us the truth and the war is really over." I said, "No, we will wait here." One of my friends said "well I am going home" and he left. By this time, my Mother was looking all over for me. She went to his home looking for me and he told her where I was. She came to the cave and found me. She told me the war was over and that we lost but I still did not believe her. I could not believe or accept this --- no way our beloved Japan could lose the war. She finally convinced me and I went home with her along with the rest of my friends. I knew at that point things would be different in Japan. But I also knew there was a reason I never made it be a kamikaze pilot or I would not be here today.

QUESTION: *It must have been a tough time during the war.*

OKAZAKI: Yes it was. There was not much food and when I was a teenager it was very difficult. Young people are always hungry. We would go

Okazaki and his college friends.

to the farms and take the food. But we would always leave a note thanking them and telling them that someday we would pay them for the food we took.

QUESTION: *Sensei, did you ever play any sports in Japan?*

OKAZAKI: You may already know this, but baseball is just as important in Japan as martial arts. It is taken very seriously. When I was teaching at the university, Nakayama Sensei came to me and said he needed a coach for the university baseball team and asked me if I knew anything about baseball. Of course I said yes, but I didn't know anything at all about it. Then he asked me if I would coach the baseball team, and not wanting to let him down, I said yes. After all, how hard could it be. After about two or three innings our team was losing. I was worried it would upset Nakayama Sensei and he would be mad at me if we lost. So I watched as the team was playing and decided they made it more difficult than it had to be. When one of our players made it to first base, it didn't make any sense to me that he would run so long around the other bases from first, to second, to third then to home plate to score. So I told the player when he got to first base and the next batter hit the ball just run directly home. Don't go to second, third, etc. It took too long and was stupid. The player said he couldn't do that and it wasn't the right way. I said, just listen to me and do what I say, I am the coach. So my player did what I told him and the umpire threw him out! I was so mad, I argued with the umpire and he argued with me back and our team lost. Nakayama Sensei found out and kicked me off the team. He said I was a terrible coach and knew nothing about baseball. He was right but it still doesn't make any sense to me.

QUESTION: *Can you tell us a little bit about your Kendo training?*

OKAZAKI: We all practiced kendo until sixth grade, every day, six days a week. The instructor was teaching kendo as a martial art, not teaching us to fight and kill. We learned the history of the Japanese samurai and then we would practice. They gave us a very short, wooden stick and we were not allowed to hit each other, just practiced the basics. I did not like this because being young we just wanted to hit each other. There are some competitive events in Kendo, and some fencing drills with a bamboo stick where you strike the head and body. We really liked that, but the instructors wouldn't let us train like that. Only basics and control. The emphasis was always that Budo is to stop the fight.

After five years, the instructor finally gave us a bamboo stick. Now we could hit each other! Oh, we loved it. But as we practiced and enjoyed striking each other, we forgot the important principle of our basics. The instructor said, "Stop. Back to the beginning --- do it again." We didn't like it, but we were made to return to basic techniques and, the wooden stick, 1 – 2, 1 – 2. Eventually, we got the bamboo sticks back, and we tried again. This time, we remembered the lessons learned during the five years of basic training.

By now, I had been training almost ten years in kendo, starting from grammar school and through middle school. Now, I advanced to using a real sword. The instructor explained how we had developed the ability to thrust our sword through the human body. The instructor did a demonstration using a bundle of bamboo sticks surrounded with straw, to be like the human body. And, he did it! He made it look so easy. With one slice of the sword he cut through the bamboo. I wanted to try it so I asked the instructor, "Can I borrow your sword?"
The instructor replied, "Don't touch my sword! It's a treasure, you know!"

That evening I went to my father who is from a Shizoku or Samurai family, and I asked him, "Sir, may I borrow your sword? My instructor said I have developed skills and abilities and I would like to test it."

IN HIS OWN WORDS

Just like my teacher, my father said, "Don't touch my sword. You have abilities --- just believe it. Don't touch my sword." But I really wanted to try. So I made a bundle of bamboo sticks wrapped it in straw. That night, I borrowed my father's sword anyway and tried it. It didn't cut through. Again I tried and it didn't cut the second time. The sword is very sharp and if you make a mistake you can damage the sword. I knew if my father saw any damages or marks he would cut off my head. I made sure to clean it and put it back where it was.

The next day I went to the instructor and said, "Sir, I tried it but the sword didn't cut through the bamboo." He looked at me and knew right away. He said, "Your mind was wrong. Don't think about cutting with your arm; use seika tanden to connect with your sword. Before you try again, close your eyes, mokuso, then say to yourself, *seika tanden, seika tanden, seika tanden,* three times. Then try it. You can do it."

One night, I tried again. I said it ten times, *seika tanden, seika tanden, seika tanden...* this time it worked. However, a Samurai always knows when someone touches his sword and my father knew when he saw his. I got in a lot of trouble for being disobedient and for touching his sword but in my mind I felt better.

QUESTION: *In comparison to Karate back then, how well organized and structured were these Martial Arts in Japan?*

OKAZAKI: In Japan in those days, all children had some form of Martial Arts in school so it was well organized and very structured. Martial Arts were a way of life, not a sport. And I always try to emphasize this to all Shotokan practitioners: never forget that we are practicing Martial Arts which is a Budo first and foremost. This is a concept that was easy for Japanese children to understand but has to be learned by non-Japanese karate-ka.

QUESTION: *Can you tell us about the history of Shotokan as you know it?*

OKAZAKI: The origin of karate dates back to about the sixth century when the Buddhist monk

IN HIS OWN WORDS

Bodhidharma traveled from India to the Shaolin Temple in China. This became Zen Buddhism. He developed exercises to make his followers strong. This evolved into Shorinji Kempo. When Zen Buddhism came to Japan in the twelfth century, these "exercises" became self-defense. From there it reached Okinawa around the fifteenth century or before. This is when it became karate. And in 1902 a commissioner of education recommended karate be included in the curriculum in schools. In 1906 Master Funakoshi (founder of modern karate) gave the first public demonstration in Okinawa. This led to his being invited to Japan in 1922 to participate in the First National Athletic Exhibition.

QUESTION: You studied directly under Gichin Funakoshi. How was the training?

OKAZAKI: Usually, Master Nakayama led the classes. Master Funakoshi would sit down and tell Nakayama Sensei what to do. He was always there observing. Master Funakoshi always stressed five important points in his teachings: the mental aspects, the physical aspects, staying calm, being exact, and being natural. He liked to explain how the human body works and how important it was to use the correct techniques to attack the right body parts.

QUESTION: *Was it the way you expected?*

OKAZAKI: No way! The training was very hard, very difficult. I recall that for the first three or four months all we did was punching techniques --- straight punches. The training sessions were up to six hours each day, six days a week. Master Funakoshi never said that we should copy his form because he understood that his body weight and his body-type made the stances and the form of the techniques that way. He was a very scientifically-minded person; don't forget that he was a school teacher. He developed the physical techniques in a certain way but he used to say, "Don't copy. Judge it by your body type."

It is very difficult to explain his movements. They looked almost without power, and more like a beautiful ballet.

He was very open-minded. For instance, he never taught us kobudo but he introduced it to us, like history. For him karate was empty-hand, but I remember him saying, "If you ever have to use a weapon, use the best one to fight with!"

QUESTION: *How many people left?*

OKAZAKI: Many of them. A lot of people left. We would stand in *kiba dachi* and punch for two hours in the morning. Then the same for another two hours in the afternoon and for another two hours in the evening. Most people just gave up. The next three months were dedicated to kicking --- just kicking techniques. After six or seven months of this kind of training, they started to combine both aspects and kata training was incorporated into the classes and became the focal point.

QUESTION: *What was the purpose of this training?*

OKAZAKI: We were like machines. This kind of training built up our muscles to an extraordinary degree. Our arms and legs were really powerful. But I didn't understand that back then. It took me over a year to see that the more hard work I put into my training the more benefits I got from it. If I missed one training session I didn't feel good at all – not my body, not my mind. But it wasn't like this in the very beginning.

QUESTION: *What do you mean?*

OKAZAKI: Well, in the very beginning I was training in kendo because kendo and judo were the common arts. I didn't enjoy judo very much, mainly because it had been thrust upon me from my early days in grammar school, so I was kind of rebellious against it. Anyway, at Takushoku University the captains from each martial art came and gave demonstrations to introduce the arts.

IN HIS OWN WORDS

QUESTION: So you were impressed with karate?

OKAZAKI: Yes, but also with aikido. I really liked them both. So I signed up for both classes.

QUESTION: **Who was the aikido teacher?**

OKAZAKI: Morihei Ueshiba himself! I was very fortunate. My karate teacher was Gichin Funakoshi and my aikido teacher was Morihei Ueshiba!

QUESTION: What are your memories of Sensei Funakoshi looking back now?

OKAZAKI: When I first started training, there was no JKA. We trained at Takushoku University. Master Funakoshi came there once a week to teach, assisted by Master Nakayama, who also taught there. The first time I saw him, I was so nervous because he was a real Grand Master. But I was so surprised because his attitude was just like a regular person; he was really nice. But I could not talk to him directly unless I got permission from Master Nakayama first. Also, Master Funakoshi was a very quiet person.

QUESTION: *Sensei Funakoshi was approximately 78 years of age when you first trained with him. How was his ability at this age, and what was his guidance to the younger karateka who would have been tempted to copy his style of movement as an older man?*

OKAZAKI: Yes, he was in his late 70s, but at that time I didn't know how old he was and I didn't think about his age. It was in the 1940s and usually 70s is an old man, but he did not look like an old man. He trained every day so he looked young. He would say, "Don't copy me," which means he knew himself. He would stand a little higher because of his age. He would explain what the stance should be, for instance *zenkutstu dachi* --- one shoulder width wide and two shoulder widths length --- the basics.

(Continued on Page 27)

Early Demonstration --Teruyuki Okazaki on the right.

Early Demonstration --Teruyuki Okazaki on the left.

Early Demonstration --- Teruyuki Okazaki on the right.

TERUYUKI OKAZAKI

Early Demonstration -- Teruyuki Okazaki on the right.

Early Demonstration -- Teruyuki Okazaki in the middle.

Early Demonstration

With Dr./Sensei Takagi -- in the middle

IN HIS OWN WORDS

Teruyuki Okazaki on the left with Hirokazu Kanazawa on the right.

Teruyuki Okazaki on the left with Masatoshi Nakayama on the right.

Teruyuki Okazaki with Katsuya Kisaka

JKA Students

TERUYUKI OKAZAKI

Teruyuki (right front) with college friends.

Photo at left:
Teruyuki Okazaki (middle) before leaving for the U.S. Masatoshi Nakayama and students seeing him off at the airport.

Photo at right:
Teruyuki Okazaki (top right) with Masatoshi Nakayama behind him, followed by Masataka Mori and Hirokazu Kanazawa

Photo at left:
Teruyuki (right) with his older brother Teruyoshi, sister-in-law Motoko, sister Keiko

Early Demonstration

Gichin Funakoshi (bottom row, far left), Masatoshi Nakayama (second row, third from left) and Hidetaka Nishiyama (second row, fourth from right), and Teruyuki Okazaki (back row, fourth from right).

Teruyuki Okazaki (back row, far left), Dr./Sensei Takagi (back row, center), and Masatoshi Nakayama (back row, far right).

(Continued from Page 21)

He would say, "Don't copy me, I am an old man. Individuals have their own body type." He had an open mind. I never thought of him as an old man; he looked young.

QUESTION: *What was the training like with Sensei Funakoshi?*

OKAZAKI: He always said, "What is real karate-do?" He would explain that we should not only develop speed and focus. He always said you have to try the best you can physically and your mind should always think about what a good martial artist is; then you are training. I try to teach this to my students as much as I can that a good martial artist follows the dojo kun and most importantly seeks perfection of character. Master Funakoshi did not say too much; technically, of course, he would explain: Do this or do that, depending on the ranking of the person. But every time, he came he taught us the most important principles technically and philosophically. And if we did something wrong, he would say, "You are not doing it the right way." I am very pleased to have studied under him.

QUESTION: *Was the term "shotokan" used to describe Funakoshi's style of karate?*

OKAZAKI: No, not at all. There was no style. Master Funakoshi just called it karate-do because he wanted it to be called karate-do. But out of respect his students started calling it "Shoto" which was Master Funakoshi's pen name. At that time, we did not have any style. We were practicing karate-do. There were times Master Nakayama wanted us to train under other karate masters, that's why he used to invite Gogen Yamaguchi from goju-kai and Hinori Otshuka from wado-ryu to teach us a different approach to the art. All these instructors gave lectures on their methods of karate and taught us various kata.

QUESTION: *Did Master Funakoshi get together with other top teachers like Master Kano or O'Sensei Ueshiba?*

OKAZAKI: Yes, of course! Master Funakoshi enjoyed very much being with Master Mifune of judo, Master Morihei Ueshiba of aikido, and Master Nakayama of kendo. They used to give demonstrations together. He always said to us that he respected very much Master Jigoro Kano's thinking of the martial arts. I know Master Kano helped Master Funakoshi when he started to teach the art of karate in Japan.

He always felt that judo had to study some karate techniques. They were very close friends and they had a lot of respect for each other.

I remember that every time we passed in front of the Kodokan, Master Funakoshi always took off his hat and bowed. "He's my teacher," he used to say. "Of course," we all answered, "But he's judo." And Master Funakoshi replied, "It doesn't matter, a martial art is martial art and I must respect it!"

IN HIS OWN WORDS

QUESTION: Sensei, you and Nishiyama Sensei trained together and both came to the United States around the same time. Were you close friends?

OKAZAKI: Yes, we were very close. We had a lot of fun together training in Japan under Sensei Nakayama. Matter of fact --- he was my best man at my wedding. Funny story: my wife Linda is American and so we got married in the U.S. I did not know anything about American marriage ceremonies. We were getting married in Las Vegas and we all drove there together in one car. Of course we had a lot of fun along the way. But the funny thing is, I was told to give the wedding ring to the best man, Mr. Nishiyama, for the ceremony. When the person conducting the ceremony said, 'Now you can place the ring on the finger,' Mr. Nishiyama handed me the ring and I took his hand and was trying to put the ring on *HIS* finger! I didn't know. I didn't understand. My wife smacked me on the arm and said, "No! The ring goes on *MY* finger!" She was so mad. But we all laughed.

QUESTION: *Sensei, when you and Sensei Nishiyama parted ways, did you get to see him much?*

OKAZAKI: Every time I went to California I would try to get together with him. The sad thing is, just before he passed away I spoke to him on the telephone and he told me he would very much like to come to our next Master Camp. I told him of course you are always welcome. And he was supposed to come to our next Master Camp but sadly he passed away just before that. I was very much looking forward to seeing him again.

Teruyuki Okazaki and wife Linda

IN HIS OWN WORDS

QUESTION: *What did your family think of you wanting to practice karate?*

OKAZAKI: My parents were not happy about it. Karate was still fairly new to Japan and they thought of it as street fighting. I was a bad kid and always fighting and getting into trouble and they thought this would make me worse. But my Grandmother who was Samurai understood martial arts talked them into it.

QUESTION: *How did you decide to concentrate on karate-do?*

OKAZAKI: It's a funny story. The training in karate classes for the first three weeks was only *usagi tobi* or "rabbit hops." Thousands of them everyday, for hours and hours. Non-stop. We would get so tired we would literally fall over on our faces, but there was Nakayama Sensei and other *senpai* to push us until we got up and kept going. I wasn't happy with that and I decided to quit. I told my roommates (their names were Irie and Onoue) that I was going to quit and concentrate on aikido training. They were my very good friends, we had been together for a long time. Pretty soon, they started to make fun of me, calling me "sissy," and saying that they would never give up. This made me so mad that I promised myself that if they could do it, I could too. So when I was going to be accepted by O'Sensei as a regular student, I stopped aikido and concentrated on karate, only to keep face with my two roommates!

QUESTION: *So what happened to them?*

OKAZAKI: Well, we were going to test for black belt under Master Funakoshi, so I was very serious about it. This time my roommates decided they wanted to quit. But I had made a promise and was pushing them to their limits in the training sessions in the early morning and in the afternoon. I insisted that they train for their test. Well, they passed their test but I flunked! Master Funakoshi said I was not good enough. My attitude was bad, very bad. I flunked many times because of it. I was a young guy thinking in the wrong direction. Master Funakoshi picked up on this right away. It was not my techniques which made me fail the test, since it was equal to the other students who passed, but my attitude. Finally I got really depressed so I went to ask Master Funakoshi

Teruyuki Okazaki and future wife, Linda, practicing for a 1962 demonstration.

why I failed the test. Of course, everybody was shocked that I actually went to speak to him. That never happens in Japanese traditional culture but I did ask Master Nakayama's permission first before I spoke to him. Master Nakayama knew why I had failed but agreed to let me speak to Master Funakoshi.

QUESTION: What did Master Funakoshi say?

OKAZAKI: He said that he really understood my problem and that he was going to tell me the essence of karate-do – but that I should be very prudent with its use. Then he sat down, and I did the same with great ceremony. I was so excited, and Master Funakoshi seemed to be really concentrating. I was nervous, and after a while he leaned over and said, "You know, Okazaki, the true essence of karate-do is to keep training --- keep training every day."

QUESTION: **Was that what you expected?**

OKAZAKI: I don't think so, but I haven't stopped training since. After that, my attitude changed and finally I got my black belt. There is an interesting story about myself right after I passed the test. I was really proud of it and Nakayama Sensei was the person in charge of teaching the beginners. One day he said, "I want you to assist me today!" Of course, I was more than pleased, I felt like a big shot. All of a

IN HIS OWN WORDS

sudden, Master Funakoshi came in and started to look around. He remembered my name because I'd been there for a long time and he asked me: "When did you pass the black belt test?" Right there I thought, "Master Funakoshi is getting old; he's getting forgetful." "Sensei, you took me for the test" I answered. Then he said, "If you are a real black belt you have to prove it. I'm sure you will be able to knock me down. Punch me or kick me. Go ahead!" I was really scared and thought, 'No way. If I touch him, my seniors will kill me right here!' The problem was that I was a very short-tempered guy and I said to myself, "OK. I might die but I have pride and I'm a black belt!" So, I attacked him in front of the whole class, with all the students and Nakayama Sensei looking on. I charged and punched at him. I thought that he was on the floor because I didn't see him in front of me when I felt somebody tapping me on the shoulder. "You need more practice Okazaki!" I don't know how he did it. My classmates said that I did a good job, but it looked as though I went through Master Funakoshi's body. Definitely, he was something special. Nakayama Sensei told me that Master Funakoshi knew how to absorb and use the attacker's energy against him.

QUESTION: *Sensei, did you ever have to take time off from training for a serious injury?*

OKAZAKI: One time I broke my leg and I told Master Nakayama I would be away from the dojo for awhile. He asked why and I told him I broke my leg and could not train. He said "So you have not learned anything." I asked him what he meant. He said "If you think you can only learn

Master Nakayama's first visit to the U.S.A./East Coast. 1968 welcome party at the Okazaki's.

by punching and kicking you do not understand karate-do. You should come to the dojo every day and watch. You will learn a lot from watching others." And that is what I did then and after that. It was frustrating not to be able to be physically training but I learned a lot about myself and from others. If I could not kick and punch due to an injury, I made sure to always be in the dojo to watch and learn. Master Nakayama's lesson was that we can always learn in all experiences no matter what.

QUESTION: *Do you ever feel a great responsibility from being one of Master Funakoshi's students?*

OKAZAKI: Yes, all the time. My generation was very fortunate to have trained under Funakoshi Sensei and to have been led by Nakayama Sensei, but I guess that no one considers themselves good enough to do the job we have to do. We were educated to believe in high quality karate-do, both technically and spiritually.

This is the only way karate can be passed down to future generations. The most important thing is that a person be a good human being. If they train hard the karate technique will happen naturally. But to be a good human being will be the best attribute to make a good martial artist.

QUESTION: *Sensei, you have a wonderful sense of humor; wasn't there an incident with Sensei Funakoshi's Cat?*

OKAZAKI: I had some years of experience, but after ten years of practice under Master Funakoshi, I was assigned a special job. I was scheduled to visit his house once a month to meet with him, exchange papers or information, and bring back his written responses. Because he was a very famous calligrapher, the senior instructors would ask me to take him papers to write something for them. Master Funakoshi would always agree and a month later I would pick up the papers, with beautiful calligraphy and his signature.

Then, one day, he invited me to have lunch at his home. I told the senior instructors about this invitation but they didn't believe me. They thought it was a joke. However, Master Funakoshi was used to my visits and knew me as one of his faithful students. As wise as he was, he could read my character and ambitions. As a member of the younger generation, he knew I was most interested in developing more speed, more focus, and getting a black belt. He was right; that was my mindset. He had been teaching us that the dojo kun was the real goal. But no, I wanted more speed and more focus. Master Funakoshi knew these thoughts were in my mind. He told me to spend more time "thinking" about the training. And I said, "Yes sir, yes sir," but on the inside, I thought, more speed, more focus. Upon my next visit, I had this experience…

Master Funakoshi's cat attacked me! Yes, he bit and scratched me, and I was unable to protect myself. That cat was a very smart animal.

Master Nakayama and all of the students in Japan took Okazaki Sensei to the airport before he left for the U.S. They all did Heian Shodan for him.

Whenever Master Funakoshi would come into the room, the cat would curl around behind him. I don't like cats, so when Master Funakoshi left the room, he'd try to come over to me but I would just smack it and the cat would jump and escape. On this occasion, as soon as Master Funakoshi left the room, the cat jumped into my lap. As I reached out to smack it, the cat bit and scratched me in one motion. I was trying to hide the blood and scratches from Master Funakoshi when he reentered the room by saying, "Oh, you have such a nice cat." He knew right away what I really thought, and that I was trying to hide the truth. He said, "What is the problem? You cannot defend yourself against my pussycat? Your mind is wrong!" You know, I still have the scar from that incident. It is a constant reminder of my reckless youth and Master Funakoshi's wisdom and guiding principles.

QUESTION: *Sensei let's talk a little about your days in College, what was the name of the university you attended and the years you were there?*

OKAZAKI: I went to Takushoku University. I was there from 1947 – 1953 when I graduated. In my generation the educational system was based on the same as England which was high school for 5 years then college for 3 years but after the war the educational system was changed to the same as the United States. But since they were changing the rules when I was there they said I could go to the college after 4 years of high school so I was the youngest in my class in college because I went there one year earlier than my classmates.

QUESTION: *May I ask what your degree was in?*

OKAZAKI: Political Economics.

QUESTION: *When did you begin training in Shotokan, college or high school?*

OKAZAKI: College in 1947. Master Gichin Funakoshi used to come to all of the colleges and universities to teach once a week. At that time Master Masatoshi Nakayama was Master Funakoshi's assistant so when Master Funakoshi was not there, Master Nakayama taught.
You know, at that time no one could go to Master Funakoshi to ask him any questions. If I had any questions I had to go to his assistant --- Master Nakayama. Those were old fashioned times, and that is one of the things I changed which is to be more accessible to my students. Before the war there were no other sports such as baseball, basketball, etc., only martial arts. It was militaristic. And the war was ending when I went to school so things were changing.

During my school years I was in the old system but when I graduated it was the new system.

QUESTION: *It must have been a confusing time for you as well as everyone else.*

OKAZAKI: Yes it was. However, even though many things were changing, martial arts never changed. Karate as a martial art never changed. At the present time it is the same as at that time. It is Budo and as you know Budo means to stop the fight, stop the conflict.

QUESTION: *Sensei, because it was the transition from the war, did it change the attitudes and way of thinking of the students then? Was the mentality different?*

OKAZAKI: Organization wise it changed. It changed to a democratic organization because before that everything was like a military. After the war we could not train in the dojo for 2 years. Martial arts training was not allowed because the authorities thought it was just for fighting.

Teruyuki Okazaki teaching at ISKF Honbu Dojo.

They did not know anything about martial arts. The Second World War was over but they thought we would want to fight but as you know the main purpose of martial arts is not to fight. General MacArthur was in Japan at that time. It is on record that all of the masters from the different martial arts --- Master Funakoshi: karate, Master Kano: Judo, Master Ueshiba: Aikido, and Master Nakayama (same name but not our Master Masatoshi Nakayama): Kendo --- went to General MacArthur and had a meeting with him to try to explain to him what the martial arts were really about and that martial arts are a culture of Japan, and that the main philosophy for martial arts is Budo which is to stop the fight, and for self-defense if someone attacks you but it is never to start a fight or conflict. Technically it looks like just kicking and punching but all the real martial arts are for peace and self-preservation. For two years General MacArthur checked what we were doing and would send the MP's (Military Police) to

come to check all the dojo's to see what we were
doing. Of course at that time we were young kids
and we liked to kick and punch and spar.
We would have someone outside watching and
if they shouted "hey, the MP's are coming" we
would stop and do kata movements. They did
not know what kata was and if they asked
we would tell them we were doing a type of
Japanese dance. After 2 years we were able
to practice martial arts again in the open.

QUESTION: *You attended Takushoku University, studying Political Economics. What was the karate club like at the time, and who was the coach?*

OKAZAKI: Yes, that was my major. Master Nakayama taught there three or four times a week. Master Funakoshi came and taught once a week, and of course Master Nakayama followed his direction on how to teach. It was about 1947 when I started at Takushoku University, and everyone was young and it was no different then.

We all thought, "Oh, I want to make speed and focus." All of those masters knew what we were thinking, and we agreed 100 percent what they were teaching but our minds were different when we first started. We just wanted speed and focus, not much philosophy; we did not think about that too much.

QUESTION: *Did you do a lot of competing in your younger years?*

OKAZAKI: When I was in college, we did not have any tournaments, not until about 1957. I started training in 1947, so for ten years we did not have any tournaments because we needed permission from Master Funakoshi to have a tournament. At that time, I was assisting Master Nakayama and we travelled around to give demonstrations to introduce what karate-do is. We also invited other dojos to come and we would train with them which was also our way of testing our skills. Then Master Nakayama began to think that if we had a tournament, we could invite all of the public to show them what karate-do is, which is one of the reasons he asked Master Funakoshi if we could have a tournament. But Master Funakoshi said no, that karate is not 100 percent sport. Master Nakayama explained to him we would bring Master Funakoshi with us and we also could put on a demonstration, and if we call it a tournament the public would become very interested and come to see it. So Master Funakoshi said if that is the reason, then yes, you can try it, but make sure that everyone follows real Martial Arts rules and regulations.

After that, for about two years, Master Nakayama studied other Martial Arts tournament rules such as Kendo, Judo, Sumo, etc. Judo and Kendo already had tournaments. Even Sumo wrestling, which is the oldest one, had tournament rules. He checked all of those rules and regulations for two years and then he made some rules, but first I had to try it out, especially for sparring. Kata was no problem because we had a point system, but sparring

IN HIS OWN WORDS

had to be analyzed to see the best way for a tournament rule, such as for one point. I did it many times to study the best way for tournament. Now our ring is square, but at that time we made it round like in Sumo, but it didn't work because the judge moves around. But then we changed it to be a square like a boxing ring. We made the rules and gave them to Master Funakoshi, who briefly read them and said, "Try it. It's not bad but try it, and if it does not work out well, then change it."

So in 1957, we had our first tournament. I wanted to participate because at that time I was assisting Master Nakayama in the Instructor Trainee Program. At that time the first instructor trainees were Masters Kanazawa and Mikami and I was teaching full-time six days a week. Our trainees were developing good technique and for the first national tournament we thought maybe they would win. Since I was teaching them, I knew each individual and if they had a special technique. So I wanted to

(Continued on Page 56)

Teruyuki Okazaki (to the left) and next to him Hirokazu Kanazawa with Masatoshi Nakayama to the far right in a demonstration for the U.S. military.

Photo right and below: *Teruyuki Okazaki.*

Left to right: Hiroshi Shirai, Hirokazu Kanazawa, Taji Kase, Keinosuke Enoeda and Teruyuki Okazaki.

IN HIS OWN WORDS

Early demonstration in the U.S.

Teruyuki Okazaki and Hidetaka Nishiyama

Teruyuki Okazaki (far left), Hiroshi Shoji (third from left), and Hidetaka Nishiyama (second from right).

Early Dan exams.

Teruyuki Okazaki and Hirokazu Kanazawa.

Early exams.

Teruyuki Okazaki (far right) and Hidetaka Nishiyama (second from right).

Teruyuki Okazaki judging.

Teruyuki Okazaki (right) and Hidetaka Nishiyama grading exams.

TERUYUKI OKAZAKI

Teruyuki Okazaki (center).

Teruyuki Okazaki (seated).

Early exams.

(Continued from Page 50)

compete because I knew their technique and thought I could win, but Master Nakayama said no, I could not compete, and we need a judge to help. So I had to be a judge. I was really disappointed. But I had to do what he said. So I never could participate as a competitor in a tournament because once you become a judge, that is it.

QUESTION: While teaching at Takushoku University, do you remember the karateka you taught there?

OKAZAKI: Mr. Ochi was a member of the team. And at that time, Mr. Kanazawa was a student there also and Mr. Habu. Then Mr. Shirai began the trainee program and when I came to the U.S. in 1961, Mr. Enoeda began the Instructor Trainee Program. When I was helping teach, Mr. Yaguchi, Mr. Mikami, and Mr. Asai were there and I had a close relationship with them. Before we began the Instructor Trainee Program, Master Nakayama instructed me on what to do technically and he had me try different things. Then he made the Instructor Trainee booklet and I was the test case. At that time, a full-time instructor trainee practiced just like we do at our Master Camp. Everyone stayed in a dormitory and we woke up at 6 AM and started training, then assisted in teaching.

QUESTION: *Can you please share some memories of the training you experienced during these years of your life?*

OKAZAKI: As I said, we were as we are now, following Master Funakoshi's principle. We had to train every day one way or another whether you wanted to or not. When I was at the Takushoku University, they had a special Martial Arts dormitory and I had to stay there with everyone and we had to get up at 6:00 a.m., start training at 6:30, then assist with teaching, and at 5:00 p.m., we had to train again before dinner, and the senior students would come and help us. We had to train a minimum of three or four times every day continuously. Full-time instructor trainees had to do that and they did not get a salary, but they got room and board until they finished the course and became full-time instructors. I was coaching Mr. Kanazawa and Mr. Ochi at that time and staying in the dormitory, and in the mornings everyone had to run. Everyone at that time was young; they were graduate students and were about 21–22 years of age and had a lot of energy. They practiced hard and in the evenings they had to go to bed at 10 PM. Of course, they were young and wanted to have some fun, have a drink, talk and get to know one another. They stayed on the second floor and the coach (me) stayed on the first floor. You know what they did? They knew if they went down the stairs I would see them, so they went out the window. I didn't know but something did not seem right; then I realized they were going out so I followed them. They went to the bar and had a couple of drinks and were having fun. That was against the rules but I did not say anything at all. Then in the morning, after that they woke up, I said, "Okay, run." Usually they had to run every morning maybe one or two laps, then back to the dojo to train. It was a warm-up. One particular morning, after two laps, they were going back to the dojo, but I said one more. Then I would say one more, and one more and one more, etc. They realized I must have found out. I could not say anything to Master Nakayama because he would have kicked them out, so I gave them this sort of punishment. Then they stopped doing that. They got the message.

Early years training in Japan with Master Nakayama.

Photos above and below: Teaching women's class in Japan.

Training with Master Nakayama.

Self defense against a knife attack.

QUESTION: *This period of time was one of great development for the art. How was this received by the wider Karate community at the time?*

OKAZAKI: When I started Karate, all of the Martial Arts were the same, to develop physically and mentally, to develop as a martial artist. But at the present time, medical science is more advanced and we have to respect that to make better development for the future. But the mental development is the same as when Martial Arts first started. Just as I always say, kata training teaches us a good balance to respect these things. When I started Karate, compared to the present time, techniques have become much more advanced because we have accepted the advice of medical science on how to develop technically. But mental development and what Martial Arts are never changes.

The principle never changes. That is why I wrote the book, *"The Textbook of Modern Karate."* It was written with a physician for sports medicine so we analyzed many things. It was 90 percent how to develop more speed and focus and to develop technically. There is nothing wrong with learning the best way to develop. But everyone has to understand what the real Shotokan Karate is. That is why I then wrote the book *"Perfection of Character,"* to make a good balance, to understand both.

QUESTION: *It has been implied that putting a more scientific emphasis on the training has taken away from the spiritual or philosophical elements of Karate. Do you think this is a fair implication?*

OKAZAKI: Different people learn in different ways. Young people are used to getting information very quickly now with computers, etc. Don't forget, the monks also were very scientific, as well as Master Funakoshi.

He understood the human body and what Karate-do could do for it. But he also had a great understanding of the human mind. He knew that modernization could bring with it many problems. Master Funakoshi could see that it could hinder the principles and goals of what Budo and Martial Arts are. This was why he gave us the Dojo Kun and Niju Kun as constant reminders of those principles. It is okay if some people find it easier to learn analyzing and use scientific means; however, it is up to all of the Sempai and instructors to remind our students of the true purpose and to teach the Dojo Kun and Niju Kun.

QUESTION: *How many forms are there in Shotokan? What are their names?*

OKAZAKI: There are fifteen basic required kata and several other optional kata. In the ISKF, we practice the kata from Master Nakayama's "Best Karate Series" books.

There are basically two categories of Shotokan kata, Shorin and Shorei. Shorin kata have quick movements with body shifting and has more speed and better suited to small, slightly built individuals. Shorei kata have slower movements and emphasize forcefulness, which contributes to the development of muscular strength. These type of kata are better suited to larger, heavily built individuals. It is important to practice both types for balanced development.

QUESTION: *How important are the styles within the art of karate?*

OKAZAKI: Karate is a complex art that requires time and dedication to fully understand. You need to dedicate time to master the basics since the art is based on the fundamental techniques. It is important that the students focus themselves in understanding their style. Karate has many different styles but in many ways all are the same. There are different 'expressions' of the art based on the different masters and their point of view. An experienced practitioner, no matter the style, will be able to understand the essentials of other karate styles if he dedicates time to study them. There are many common points in all styles but I strongly disagree with

Teruyuki Okazaki, his nephew Hiroyoshi and Hiroyoshi's daughter Kiyomi.

the approach of practicing two styles or different methods. That will only lead to confusion.

I have thought that ultimately, simplification is the best path to mastery. Grand Master Funakoshi only had 15 fundamental kata in the Shotokan style. There was a reason for it. Karate mastery is not about the accumulation of forms and techniques.

QUESTION: *But other kata were added afterwards, correct?*

OKAZAKI: Yes, it is true. But I don't think that karate mastery lies in how many numbers of kata the student knows. Goju Ryu has only about a dozen, Shorin Ryu around the same, etc. Accumulation is not the key to mastery but the focus on the technical refinement of a few things. Think of kumite... if you have a good solid set of 4-5 techniques that you can use at will and against anybody...you won't need more. It is better to know well 10 techniques that you can use anytime and against anybody than 1,000 that you can't apply.

Unfortunately, many people judge the level of the practitioner by the number of kata that they know. When Grand Master Funakoshi went to Tokyo, people used to ask him how many kata he knew. He used to answer like 50-60 kata. Maybe he knew all these in a perfect order but he also knew that the purpose of kata training is not the accumulation of fighting techniques --- sequences in a certain order. Grand Master Funakoshi was very aware that Okinawan masters only knew a few kata and dedicated all their lives to master those few. Kata was the original way to practice karate in the old days. In karate we go from kata to bunkai to kumite but it is interesting to note that after a certain age, if we don't practice kata we can't simply practice karate anymore.

QUESTION: *What do you think about the changes in kata for competition purposes?*

OKAZAKI: I don't agree with that. Kata should not be altered for competition. We should not exaggerate movements or change the techniques to better fit the competition format. They do this to impress the judges. The question is "Why should the judges be impressed if they know real (and not fancy) karate?"

Kata training has evolved throughout the years. Originally some kata changed and maybe some parts were left incomplete. We don't know, but we still practice the way Nakayama Sensei taught. Constant repetition is necessary to digest the movements. We need to do the same movements thousands of times to really absorb them. I recommend to train kata not only in the dojo but also on different kinds of terrain like grass, sand and even rocky places. Kata is self-defense and this kind of training will help the practitioner to better understand the form and the physical action that he is performing.

QUESTION: *How many times do you have to do a kata to really "make it your own"?*

OKAZAKI: That is hard to say but after you do one kata 1,000 times, it will substantially improve. After 2,000 the movements it will be really powerful and real and the timing and rhythm of the kata is coming to life. And after 5,000 times, we can say that you are making the kata your own. Of course, these are just a guideline number and it depends on the student's ability to learn. Think of a single technique like a 'gyaku-tsuki': if you do it 1,000 times you don't master that technique at all [it can be done in one single training session]…but maybe after 10,000 times you know it well and it becomes a 'reflex' to be used in a real self-defense situation. Kata is not different! Also, keep in mind that everyone has a different body type, and one person's kata will not look exactly like the other person's. It should be technically correct, but there are differences in age, athleticism, etc. And this is more true as we age, an older person's kata will not look like a young person, but again, it must be technically correct. That is also why I say karate is a lifetime endeavor – it takes your entire life to fully understand kata.

QUESTION: *What is your favorite kata, Sensei?*

OKAZAKI: Heian Shodan. I am still learning Heian Shodan and it still challenges me. And I also end every class, especially our advanced Black Belt class with Heian Shodan. I say to the black belts, ok now do your favorite kata.

And they know by now that I am telling them to do Heian Shodan. It is important to keep the mindset "Shoshin ni kaeru" or back to the beginning. We must always understand that when we have the beginner mind we are open to learning and this is very true of Heian Shodan.

QUESTION: *What about all the differences in styles. Do you think they separate practitioners?*

OKAZAKI: Absolutely. Every practitioner thinks their style is the best. This is an attitude that I don't like.

QUESTION: *Why?*

OKAZAKI: Because it is not true. Shotokan is not better than other style and others styles are not better than Shotokan. They are different expressions of the same art. In Shotokan, we emphasize certain aspects in a certain way and in other styles they emphasize other elements, or even the same, but in a different way.

ISKF Headquarters -- Philadelphia, PA, U.S.A.

IN HIS OWN WORDS

***QUESTION:** How is the body aligned in Shotokan?*

OKAZAKI: Alignment begins with correct body posture. This must be maintained at all times. And we also stress correct stance. Stances are what gives the practitioner stability, balance and mobility. There are many different stances in Shotokan depending on tension of the knees whether it is inward or outward, foot position, etc., but the basic principle remains the same. If you have a strong stance then your foundation will be strong which will give more body power and movement.

Early demonstration in Japan.

QUESTION: *Sensei, did you try other martial arts besides Shotokan karate at that time?*

OKAZAKI: Yes, at that time martial arts were mandatory. In grammar school before the war, it was mandatory to practice Kendo. Kendo is the oldest Japanese martial art. The instructor always explained to us what a real martial art is; however, we were young and didn't listen. We just wanted to hit each other (Master Okazaki laughs and displays a glimmer of youthful mischievousness). But in martial arts you never fight anybody. I practiced Kendo for five years then when we went to middle

Empi uchi!

school we could choose which martial art we wanted to study. As I said, Kendo is the oldest martial art in Japan and that is why they taught it in grammar school. And not just technique, they also taught how to bow correctly and those kind of things. If you did not do those things correctly the teacher would yell at you. Then in high school I tried Judo. I didn't like it very much so I went back to Kendo again. I studied Kendo for 10 years. Then, when I went to the university I studied Aikido. A friend of mine was doing it and so I tried it and studied with Master Ueshiba. I went every day and tried the best I could. Then one day Master Ueshiba called me over. He knew why I was training and said get out. I was trying the best I could so I got very mad inside. Then I saw a karate demonstration and I thought it was the best fighting technique and I'm going to study karate and challenge Master Ueshiba. I was just a kid.

QUESTION: **Sensei, when you were in the university were there any rivalries with other colleges or universities?**

OKAZAKI: Yes, we did not have tournaments at that time but we would have a shiai or special type of goodwill training. We had that kind of special training sparring with the other universities. And of course we wanted to beat the other teams. At that time Master Funakoshi was against tournaments because he said it is not a sport, it is a martial art. So we would have a shiai with all of the universities and we would travel all around Japan.

QUESTION: **Was karate an accredited course in the university?**

OKAZAKI: Yes it was.

QUESTION: **How many people did they have in the class usually?**

OKAZAKI: It depended on the university but I would say a minimum of 50 – 100. When it became one of the subjects for physical education many young people became interested. They already knew Judo, Kendo, and Aikido so this was fairly new because as you know Master Funakoshi brought it to Japan from Okinawa.

QUESTION: *Were there women in class at that time?*

OKAZAKI: At that time they did not accept women in the karate class. Women and men trained separately in martial arts. Women mostly practiced Naginata (stick fighting). When I started teaching here at Temple University in the United States, the university thought it was like sports and suggested that I separate the women and the men. I told them no, we are a martial art and also if a woman is attacked on the street it would most likely be by a man so she needs to learn how to defend herself against men. So the university said ok we will try it that way and after they watched my classes at the university they agreed that this is different from sports and from then on the men and women trained together.

QUESTION: *What are the most important differences between the "old" way of training and nowadays?*

OKAZAKI: It is important to remember that we were a group of karateka that came right after World War II. Japan was under a lot of the post-war pressure and the "warrior mentality" was present in everything in the society.
Everything we did was done with that "spirit". Therefore, the karate training was based on strong spirit. We had that mentality because the way society was at that moment. Karate training for us was a matter of surviving; thousands of punches and thousands of kicks in every practice. To be honest I must say that "spirit was first, then technique". We built our karate on "spirit". To punch 10,000 times you need more than a strong body. A strong body won't take you "there". It is your spirit. You use it to push the

(Continued on Page 88)

IN HIS OWN WORDS

Teruyuki Okazaki; early East Coast Championship.

Teruyuki Okazaki (photos right and below)

Teruyuki Okazaki and Masatoshi Nakayama --- ISKF Master Camp, U.S.A.

TERUYUKI OKAZAKI

Photo right:
Teruyuki Okazaki --- teaching.

Photo below:
Teruyuki Okazaki in ISKF Honbu Dojo.

Photo above:
Teruyuki Okazaki --- impeccable form

Photo left:
Teruyuki Okazaki celebrating a birthday at ISKF Master Camp, USA.

IN HIS OWN WORDS

Photo below:
Teruyuki Okazaki in an early demonstration (notice the response of the spectator in the back!).

Teruyuki Okazaki (above photo) and Okazaki enjoying a rare free moment (photo below).

Photo above:
Teruyuki Okazaki --- always time to say hello even in his busiest moments.

TERUYUKI OKAZAKI

Photo right:
Teruyuki Okazaki --- experiencing all cultures.

Photo below:
Katsuya Kisaka.

Photo right:
Teruyuki Okazaki --- Shofuso, Philadelphia, PA, U.S.A.)

Photos this page:
Teruyuki Okazaki in demonstration with Ronald Johnson.

TERUYUKI OKAZAKI

Photos this page:
Teruyuki Okazaki seminar.

IN HIS OWN WORDS

Photo at right:
Teruyuki Okazaki teaching.

Photo below:
Teruyuki Okazaki at ISKF Master Camp, Camp Green Lane, PA.

Teruyuki Okazaki (above photo), proud of passing the legacy of his instructors through his book "Perfection of Character."

Teruyuki Okazaki (above photo) --- always making the youth feel just as important as the adults, and (right) Shomen --- ISKF Honbu Dojo, Philadelphia, PA, U.S.A.

TERUYUKI OKAZAKI

Photo at right:
Teruyuki Okazaki --- yoko geri kekomi.

Photo below:
Teaching punching using Seika Tanden.

Photo at right: *Mawashi Geri.*
Below left: *Preparation for side kick*
Below right: *Teaching at ISKF Honbu Dojo, Philadelphia, PA.*

IN HIS OWN WORDS

(Continued from Page 79)

body beyond natural limits and eventually your technique will become extremely strong... as a by-product of your "warrior spirit".

This method of thinking can carry you through your hardships in your every day life. If your spirit can get you through a difficult class like that, then your spirit is training to tackle any obstacle in your life.

QUESTION: *Do you think that is lacking in our modern days?*

OKAZAKI: To some extent yes, definitely.

We have a more relaxed and comfortable society. If I get to the dojo and have the students punch "gyaku-tsuki" for the full hour every class for a week....probably nobody will show up for class the next week!

It is a different generation, different society, different goals and different beliefs. Part of that is the computer age, people are used to getting information and whatever they need with the click of a button. They watch videos on the computer and think this is training. Nothing is wrong with seeking more information and doing research, but nothing can replace the physical aspect. If you push your body to its limit, your spirit will follow and you are achieving a higher level of martial arts.

QUESTION: *Is it better or worse?*

OKAZAKI: Let's say that is "different" and leave it at that.

QUESTION: *You were always recognized for your amazing kicking ability. Were you a natural kicker?*

OKAZAKI: I always try to follow Master Funakoshi's principle. He said in daily life, you do not use the legs much, just for walking. The hands, yes, they are already coordinated. He said that is why you have to practice leg techniques 50 percent more than hand techniques. If you do punching 10 times, then you should do 15–20 kicking techniques.

That is what I followed and it makes a good balance. Yes, kicking techniques can have more power than hand techniques and we studied how much different they are. Kicking techniques are stronger and that is why I followed Master Funakoshi's advice and practiced kicking techniques more --- to help them to develop. As he said, have a good balance. Of course it depends on the distance when you are defending yourself. Maybe kicking would be more effective, or punching would be more effective. He said it doesn't make any difference, but you have to practice kicking techniques more to develop coordination. That is what he said and that is why I did it. Of course, each individual has something he or she is better at; maybe someone is better at kata or another person may have stronger punching techniques. But I practiced kicking more than anyone else and that is why. Everything must be balanced.

Good kicking is based on tedious repetition of the basic techniques and although I always

Yoko Geri Kekomi - perfect!

had good flexibility, it is not a requirement for effective kicking.

Flexibility is important because it allows us to kick more smoothly and with less effort. Its training is greatly exaggerated and largely misunderstood. Not everybody can achieve the same levels of flexibility because it depends on the age, physical background, previous training, etc. Flexibility training should be treated as simply another integral part of the overall karate training and conditioning. During all my years of training, I have seen many practitioners dedicating too much time and effort trying to achieve full splits. We have to be careful though.

By stretching too much, the muscle becomes too long and possibly too soft. This will prevent the practitioner from using their body fully to produce power in the techniques. Ligaments and tendons will get weaker with over-stretching. We need to find the right point and not push it too much. Dynamic tension can help to counter balance the negative effects of too much stretching. But gentle stretching must be done every day to keep the ligaments from tightening.

QUESTION: *In 1955, alongside Master Nakayama, you helped develop the Instructor Program. Do you remember what the primary goals were in developing this program?*

OKAZAKI: Master Nakayama followed Master Funakoshi's principles, technically and philosophically, and everything. He taught us that when we taught we should think about our members, which is the most important philosophy. Of course, when Master Nakayama was developing the Instructor Trainee Program, he changed a couple of things to make them better.

QUESTION: *What were the most important skills that you wanted to give the graduating instructors?*

OKAZAKI: Shotokan karate is a Martial Art and a real Martial Art means never to fight. Master Funakoshi said karate is never to attack first. That is the most important principle. Of course, if someone is trying to kill you, you must defend yourself. That is what karate's techniques are for: to defend yourself, but never attack first. Or maybe some crazy person tries to attack someone else, you have to help them. It is not only karate, but all Martial Arts. It is not to fight; Martial Arts are to stop the fight or stop the conflict. It is a way of life that is the real Martial Art. When you analyze the kata, they give us very important principles technically and philosophically. When you analyze all of the kata movements, all of those masters studied these kata and told us it is a lifetime of training, and they gave us this message that this is karate's techniques and philosophies. So I always say, when you analyze the kata and even techniques, 60 percent of techniques are blocking techniques. Why blocking? If someone attacks you have to hit, but why block? They say it is to stop the fight. Those are the things they are teaching us. That is why everyone has to understand that blocking techniques must be strong because they are also striking techniques. You must stop the fight and you do not have to knock them down. That is why kata is a very important principle to karate's techniques.

QUESTION: Could you please share some memories or stories from the time in your life where you were developing the program?

OKAZAKI: I am a really lucky guy to have studied under Master Funakoshi and Master Nakayama, to observe their ideas and their philosophies. My experience was that when you are young, after we started tournaments, everyone would like to be a champion. Nothing is wrong with that; it makes everyone train harder to develop their technique physically, but mentally they have to think why they are training. After the tournament, the instructor's minds also change. They think they would like to make their student a champion. The teaching method changes, how to get a point especially for sparring. Then Master Nakayama got upset. He came every year to our ISKF Master Camp until he passed away. We would have a meeting and he would say, "we have to change some rules and how to teach because look at how their attitudes are changing. It is not a real Martial Art anymore." So those are some of things we would discuss: how to change some rules, etc., even how to bow; if their attitude is bad, they should lose right away. Tournaments can help by motivating people to train harder; they will get a lot of benefit. But it is the instructor's responsibility to remind their students why they are training. After tournaments, they stop training. The same thing happens with ranking. When they are working toward the black belt, they train harder; when they pass, they stop training. That is why we have a rule here at honbu dojo; we wait one year before they get their certificate. If they do not train, they do not get a certificate. They must practice continuously. Then they understand why they are training. I always say, tournaments are the same as dojo training. It is a special type of dojo training. That is Master Funakoshi and Master Nakayama's important principle --- everything is dojo training.

QUESTION: *How did Master Jigoro Kano influence the ranking system in Karate?*

OKAZAKI: Master Kano was a very famous Judo master and he was very close with Master Funakoshi and he suggested that times were changing and if you have a ranking system students would train harder. So Master Funakoshi agreed and he started the ranking system. From the nineteenth to the twentieth century many things changed, but the principle is exactly the same and we still keep it. But the training method is different. In our time, for one

A rare moment at the seashore relaxing --- but always an avid reader

month we may have done only punching, one month only kicking, those kind of things. Then medical science analyzed things: the best way to develop the body; if you train this way or that way, you can make more speed and focus. But a long time ago, it was more mental development when practicing the techniques. Now, we have to have a balance of both mental and physical. That is why we have a tournament, to develop both of those things. But sometimes some people only think one way, to develop for a tournament or ranking system. This is wrong; Master Funakoshi would say that is not training.

QUESTION: *You taught the very first batch of instructors in the Instructor Program, including Hirokazu Kanazawa, Takayuki Mikami, etc. What do you remember of the success and weaknesses of the course in its first year, and were there any revisions to the program for the second batch of students in the Kenshusei?*

OKAZAKI: The first batch was sort of a test case. As I said, I stayed in the dormitory with them and every morning we had running and training and I would push them harder to teach them, and I would report to Master Nakayama how they were doing. After the training, they had to study and write a report every week. And Master

Nakayama would ask them why they wrote this or said that. After that, when they had the knowledge and ability, we would give them a written and physical test and they would become official instructors. After that, we planned to send them overseas. Mr. Mikami was being sent to the Philippines and Mr. Kanazawa went to Hawaii to teach. So those two got some experience outside of Japan and when they came back they gave a report. After that, the second group was Mr. Yaguchi, Mr. Asai, Mr. Yamaguchi, and Mr. Shirai, and they did it exactly the same.

QUESTION: *When you first developed tournaments with Master Nakayama, did you see a difference in the way the students trained?*

OKAZAKI: When we first developed the tournament it was just for demonstration purposes. We traveled all over to do this but then after 2 years Master Nakayama explained to Master Funakoshi if we have an event here and invite all of the public everyone can come to see it. It is a small island and easily accessible. That was one of the reasons. We got Master Funakoshi's permission to do it, sparring and kata but he said to make sure there are rules. After the 2 years Master Nakayama tested out many different rules but the most important rule was never to make contact. Martial arts are never to start the fight. It is good to test your skills in sparring and kata but never make contact. At that time Mr. Mikami, Mr. Kanazawa, and others were all instructor trainees and were going to be in the first tournament. It was 1957. I wanted to participate to test my skills but Master Nakayama said no, I need your help to judge. I was disappointed but had to judge. In the tournament there was a lot of kicking and punching and not enough rules. Then Master Nakayama said we better change the rules to make them stricter. Master Funakoshi agreed to have the tournaments as a way to show the public what karate was about and also just like ranking tests it would motivate the students to train harder. Anything that made students train harder would give them a benefit.

Unfortunately, some instructors began to teach how to make a champion and Master Nakayama began to notice that and every year when he came to Master Camp he would tell me to change the tournament again. But one rule we will never change is that tournaments are good to test your skills but they are just like dojo training. That is why we line up, do seiza, bow and again at the end of the tournament and always say the Dojo Kun.

QUESTION: **How would you describe your relationship with Master Nakayama?**

OKAZAKI: He would come to the college three or four times a week and I had the same experience with him as with Master Funakoshi. They could read my mind that I was thinking only about how to improve speed and focus. Master Nakayama always followed Master Funakoshi's direction. After I graduated, Master Nakayama picked me to coach the team, and every time he went somewhere I would ask him if I could go with him. One time, he went to Thailand and I went with him. He invited the Thai government to come and watch because Thai boxing was a little different from Karate and he wanted them to see it. We put on a demonstration and they said, "Oh, that is a little different." Thai boxing did not have techniques like Karate's kicking and punching techniques. They wanted to have a competition with a Thai boxer and me. So I went every day to watch how they boxed. After observing them, I knew which kind of techniques they did not have, so I thought, "I can knock them down!" Then I spoke to Master Nakayama and I told them, yes, I can accept and I can fight. He said you cannot do that; that would not be fair. There have to be some kind of rules. Then they came and said you can't do this or you can't do that. Master Nakayama said we have to be able to use all of Karate's techniques. The said, okay, we could make a rule that you can use this technique or that technique. Then Master Nakayama said okay. Master Nakayama and I put on a Karate demonstration and they sent the champion of Thai boxing, who put on a demonstration of their techniques. The newspaper came and took pictures and then they wrote a story about it. I could not read it but I found out that they wrote that a Karate master came over from Japan to challenge the Thai boxer. Then one day, Master Nakayama and I were walking down the street and a young kid

Teruyuki Okazaki

came up and said, oh, you are the Karate master and he kicked at Master Nakayama's head. The next thing I knew, the kid was lying in the street. Master Nakayama said: "do not say anything; let's go right away." This was just like Master Funakoshi, no one could touch them. I didn't say anything but now he is upstairs, so I can say it. Almost any place he went, I went with him – practice, demonstrations, etc. He was like an older brother or father to me. I used to stay at his house and Mrs. Nakayama would take care of me.

QUESTION: *Did Sensei Nakayama come to your Master Camp?*

OKAZAKI: Yes, every year he came to the U.S. to come to our Master Camp. He loved it because he still felt close to us and we remained his students. However, when he got sick, his wife called me to tell me he was in the hospital. I went there to see him and he said "I am very sorry I cannot come to camp this year." I told him it was ok and we would continue to come to see him. But 2 days later Mrs. Nakayama called me to tell me he had passed away. I still miss him and hope I am doing what he would have wanted.

QUESTION: *Do you think Sensei Nakayama's vision of the future is the reason Shotokan Karate is so internationally popular today?*

OKAZAKI: Master Nakayama travelled around the world and he understood different cultures. He knew we had to keep our principles while at the same time respecting other people's cultures and differences. I think that is one of the main reasons he was so well accepted around the world and was able to spread Karate-do to these other countries. Even now, I know from travelling around the world myself that other countries appreciate that we accept their differences and at the same time they do their best to maintain the Japanese tradition within Shotokan Karate.

IN HIS OWN WORDS

QUESTION: *Why did you decide to move to the United States?*

OKAZAKI: Master Funakoshi's last years were taken up with instruction and preparation to send instructors all over the world. In 1953 we did a nationwide US tour for judo and karate. After that tour, Master Funakoshi received a lot of letters asking for instructors, so they sent me over in 1961. This was supposed to be for only six months. After 6 months I asked if I could come back to Japan, and Master Nakayama said not yet. Then each year I would ask again and again he would say not yet. And here I am, 57 years later I am still here and this is my home.

When I first came to the United States there was a big problem. I couldn't speak a word of English. It was terrible for me. They sent me to Philadelphia because they thought it was a more convenient location. Anyway, the major problem with that plan was my English! You know, in the beginning I couldn't read the menus at the restaurants so I used to point at something.

It could be soup or chicken, or steak. I had a very hard time. When I learned how to say French fries, I ordered a lot of French fries all the time because it was all I could say. But my English improved thanks to my wife. Like karate training! The most important thing is do your best. Not only in karate but in everything you do in your life. We are all human beings, there is no way we can be perfect. But the idea of getting better and better every day is what's important. Just do your best. And I met my wife when I was teaching at Temple University and she also helped me tremendously to understand the language and American culture.

QUESTION: *Have you found that your teaching has changed over the last forty years?*

OKAZAKI: Before I came to the U.S.A., Mr. Kosaka, who was the president of the Japan Karate Association and the Japan Foreign Minister, hosted a farewell party for all the

IN HIS OWN WORDS

senior instructors. He came to me and said, "Okazaki, the first thing you have to do is to have some friends who are lawyers and doctors." At that moment, I didn't understand what he meant. Now I do. When I came to this country I tried my best to make people understand karate-do, I had to be strict – but have control at the same time. You cannot be physically abusive. I always used a *shinai* stick but it depends on how you use it. If you hit hard it is not good, but sometimes it is good to make a loud sound so the students wake up. Think about it as an instructional method. Times and society have changed both here and in Japan. The basics are the same because we are human beings but the mental attitude has changed. Students think that if they pay this much, they must get that much. That's what they believe and we can't blame them because they are like part of a machine. The youth don't practice how to think. Karate-do or other physical discipline teaches them that if you don't sweat and work really

(Continued on Page 114)

Photo above (left to right): *Teruyuki Okazaki, Hideki Okamoto, Takayuki Mikami, Shigeru Takashina --- ISKF Master Camp.*

Teruyuki Okazaki with Shigeru Takashina (photo above); with Tetsuhiko Asai (left); and (photo below) Teruyoshi Okazaki (on far left) with his brother.

IN HIS OWN WORDS

Photo left:
Masahiko Tanaka, Shibasaki, Teruyuki Okazaki, and Yutaka Yaguchi.

Photo below:
Yutaka Yaguchi, Teruyuki Okazaki and Takayuki Mikami.

Photo below: *Teruyuki Okazaki*

Photo at page bottom:
Shojiro Koyama, Yutaka Yaguchi, Teruyuki Okazaki, and Takayuki Mikami.

TERUYUKI OKAZAKI

Photo left:
Teruyuki Okazaki (second from right), Yukichi Tabata (far right), Masatoshi Nakayama (seated).

Photo below right:
Teruyuki Okazaki and Yutaka Yaguchi.

Photo below left:
Teruyuki Okazaki and Yutaka Yaguchi (one can only imagine what Master Yaguchi said to make Grand Master Okazaki laugh).

Photo below: *Standing (left to right): Shojiro Koyama, Masatoshi Nakayama, Teruyuki Okazaki, Yutaka Yaguchi and Shigeru Takashina; Front row: James Field, Greer Golden and Ronald Romano.*

IN HIS OWN WORDS

Photo at left:
Teruyuki Okazaki (left).

Middle photo
(left to right):
Teruyuki Okazaki, Motokuni Sugiura, and Yutaka Yaguchi.

Bottom photo:
Masatoshi Nakayama, Teruyuki Okazaki, Masataka Mori, Keinosuke Enoeda, Taji Kase, and Tetsuhiko Asai.

TERUYUKI OKAZAKI

Photo at right:
Teruyuki Okazaki and his mother, Tsuneko.

Middle right photo:
Teruyuki Okazaki and Masatoshi Nakayama.

Middle left photo:
Teruyuki Okazaki always enjoys speaking to everyone and sharing his philosophy.

Bottom photo:
Dinner with Master Masatoshi Nakayama (at center).

(Continued from Page 108)

hard for something, you'll never get anything. But if I used the same teaching methods that I did forty years ago, I wouldn't have any students!

QUESTION: *Did you finish your studies in the Takushoku University?*

OKAZAKI: Yes, I did.

QUESTION: *When did you become an official JKA instructor?*

OKAZAKI: I guess the Japan Karate Association was officially organized around 1955. So I was hired as an assistant instructor and quit the job I had. I became the first coach at the instructor's course. Master Nakayama had plans to make official instructors and I became a kind of guinea pig, because he used to give me several projects to study, practice and report on. He analyzed everything I gave him and later on he started the official instructors program. Like I said, I became a coach to the instructor trainees. The first

graduate was Mr. Mikami, and then
Mr. Kanazawa, and Mr. Takakura. The idea was that becoming a karate instructor was to be the equal of studying the curriculum in a university to become a teacher. We had courses on how to teach the techniques, how to practice by yourself, and on subjects like physics, scientific aspects, et cetera. One of the prerequisites was a degree from a 4-year college. So this course became sort of a Master's degree.

QUESTION: *Do you consider karate to be a sport?*

OKAZAKI: No. Karate-do is Budo, and Budo is not a sport. The real meaning of Budo is to go into life more deeply and improve physical and spiritual qualities through hard training. The essence or concept of sport is to get away from the toils of life and have some fun. Master Funakoshi was against tournaments but I remember Nakayama Sensei telling him that it was a good way to promote the art and introduce it to the public. Nakayama Sensei stressed that it is not about trophies and medals but to bring the art into the public eye. Master Jigoro Kano also recommended that Master Funakoshi have a ranking system as a motivational tool. These old masters were training for personal development and didn't need these kind of external rewards. But the times changed and people think and train for different reasons. The environment and the economic situations are all very different. But these masters reached a very high level with the old methods. That's why I keep training --- to reach their level of excellence. That's the real challenge for the modern martial artists.

QUESTION: *Are you against karate being accepted in the Olympics?*

OKAZAKI: I would like to see what Nakayama Sensei suggested before passing away --- the Budo Olympics. All Budo arts together, exchanging techniques and training methods where there are no winners or losers. This would return us to the original concept of Budo and we could educate people about the art and the true meaning of the Way of the Warrior. Nakayama Sensei said to me, "We must make people understand the true martial arts way." And this is what I'm trying to do, and the very reason why even after a tournament we still do the dojo kun.

College friends --- Teruyuki Okazaki, standing at far right.

QUESTION: *What is your opinion about karate entering in the Olympic Games?*

OKAZAKI: Karate is not a sport. Karate is like a 1,000 page book. The sportive aspect it is just a chapter...like 40-50 pages. That chapter only is nothing without the rest of the pages. It is also limited for the young. Karate is an art, a self-defense method, a philosophy, a way of life. Just as Nakayama Sensei felt, I am also afraid that the sport will be emphasized too much and many other aspects of karate will be lost and left behind. Olympic Games can bring a bigger exposure for the younger generation but if the teacher does not teach the whole art of karate as it is...then it will be not good for the art.

QUESTION: *How should we approach the sport aspect of karate?*

OKAZAKI: Competition is a growing experience. That is what it really is. You learn better timing with your techniques, you have the opportunity of facing opponents that you don't know, you learn how to read the action of an unknown opponent, you learn to adapt to the competition environment which is very different than the dojo and you learn how to handle the pressure and face fear, etc.

The important aspect is the "participation side of it and its benefits and not the final victory".

QUESTION: *It sounds like the "ideal" of Baron Pierre de Coubertin, founder of the Modern Era Olympic Games.*

OKAZAKI: Yes. He conceived the Olympic ideals for the sport as a vehicle for human growth and individual development where winning was not the main and important thing. It was the development of the individual in the society that was his final goal. Like Funakoshi Sensei said; "the ultimate aim of karate lies not in victory nor defeat, but in the perfection of the character of its participants". Budo and sports are different but both men had a very similar approach to what those things really should be.

Unfortunately, what we have today (in both karate and Olympic Games) is very different. That is the danger for karate --- that practitioners focus on competition, sport and medals and not in the overall value and philosophy of karate.

QUESTION: *Sensei, what is your opinion about other combat forms of karate like Full Contact and other modern sports?*

OKAZAKI: I guess they are alright if we take them like sports...not like a form of martial arts. Karate is not a sport, so I don't look at what we practice as a sportive activity that we can compare to boxing, kickboxing or Full Contact. Karate is a complete art that offers us the possibility of having a friendly exchange in a competition format. Combat sports are alright if that is what the individual wants to do but karate-do is much more than fighting and much more than sport competition.

QUESTION: *Did Master Funakoshi ever get involved in grappling or throwing techniques at all?*

OKAZAKI: Yes, he did. In fact he explained that many of the kata applications, the *bunkai* were throwing techniques. But he always stressed that before you throw your opponent to the floor you must punch or kick in order to finish them first. He liked to throw the opponent in front of the next attacker, using him as a kind of protective shield.

QUESTION: ***Do you try to preserve Master Funakoshi's and Sensei Nakayama's teachings and philosophy?***

OKAZAKI: That's my goal and purpose. Nakayama Sensei was like a father to me --- sometimes like an older brother who was always there helping me and guiding me. Master Funakoshi was like a grandfather. I must fulfill my obligation to my original teachers. Karate-do was taught by Master Funakoshi and Master

Left to right: *Teruyuki Okazaki, Shojiro Koyama, Takayuki Mikami and Shigeru Takashina --- ISKF Master Camp.*

Nakayama as a way of life. He gave us, his proteges, the *Shoto Ni Ju Kun* or "20 Precepts to Live By." The idea of those is that karate-do is Budo and its goal is to develop character in human beings and to avoid conflicts.

QUESTION: *Is getting a black belt the ultimate goal of karate-do?*

OKAZAKI: Not at all. A black belt is just the beginning of a journey. It is a degree of skill but not of ability or understanding of the teaching methods. These are two very different things. I strongly emphasize to my instructors to be patient. To understand. It's important that the instructor knows how to communicate and "give" something to the student so we create a better society. Karate training is not easy when practiced correctly. You must challenge yourself not to give up. When you challenge yourself you are training your spirit. When you force yourself never to give up, you are training your spirit. Some people think of getting a black belt like a graduation. They are finished. It is the exact opposite. It is the beginning, you are now ready to learn. And it is at this point that you should give back to your dojo by sharing your knowledge and helping beginners. The dojo is not like a gym where you go to work out then leave. Dojo is translated to mean the place where we go to study the way. We are always studying and learning in the dojo and sharing techniques and principles.

QUESTION: *Do you have any advice for anyone interested in learning more styles?*

OKAZAKI: It is my personal opinion that there is no time to study other styles. It takes a lifetime to study Shotokan. If we train seriously we continue to learn that the simplest techniques can be complex and vice versa. Also, every kata, from Heian Shodan on up is complex. Kata alone take a lifetime to understand and fully appreciate. The more you do Heian Shodan as you advance you realize how difficult it can be.

IN HIS OWN WORDS

This is why it is so important to continue to study your basics and all the katas no matter what rank you become.

QUESTION: *Do you have any plans to go back to Japan?*

OKAZAKI: My teacher sent me over here in 1961, so here I am. I was ready to go back anytime they decided, but it didn't happen.

Unfortunately, both of them have passed away. Compared to them, I am nothing. I hope they feel proud of me wherever they are now.

QUESTION: *Do you think karate-do keeps you young?*

OKAZAKI: Daily training gives you vitality, energy, and health. Keep training! Keep training! We can never reach perfection, but we must keep training. That's my challenge and responsibility as Master Funakoshi's student and a teacher of his philosophy.

TERUYUKI OKAZAKI

Photo at right:
Teruyuki Okazaki loved the sun!

Middle left photo:
Teruyuki Okazaki --- early days in U.S.A.

Middle right photo:
Teruyuki Okazaki demonstration with Paul White and Ronald Johnson.

Bottom photo
(left to right): *Shigeru Takashina, Shojiro Koyama, Takayuki Mikami, Yutaka Yaguchi, Teruyuki Okazaki and Tetsuhiko Asai --- grading at ISKF Master Camp.*

Top photo (Left to right): *Hideo Ochi, Yutaka Yaguchi, Teruyuki Okazaki, Keinosuke Enoeda and Shigeru Takashina --- ISKF Master Camp.*

Photo at right: *Teruyuki Okazaki (second from right).*

Bottom photo: *Teruyuki Okazaki center, Greer Golden (to left) and Yutaka Yaguchi (standing) --- ISKF Master Camp.*

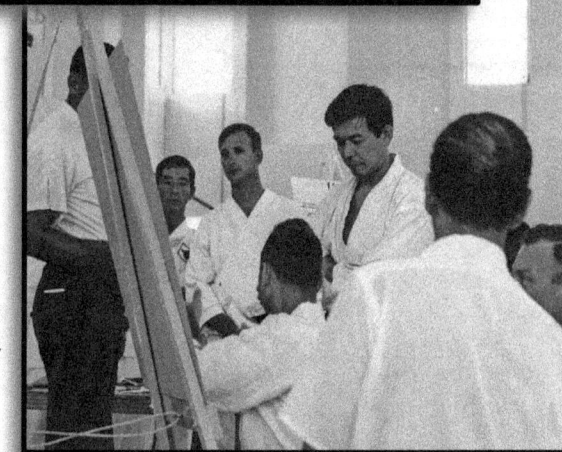

TERUYUKI OKAZAKI

Above photo:
Early knife demonstration --- Katsuya Kisaka (left) and Teruyuki Okazaki (right).

Photo at left:
Teruyuki Okazaki ---ISKF Master Camp, always preferring to look directly in the eyes.

Photo at right:
A tree was planted in honor of Teruyuki Okazaki at Camp Green Lane, U.S.A. --- site of the ISKF Master Camp.

IN HIS OWN WORDS

Top photo: *Robert Sandler (standing, far left), Teruyuki Okazaki (standing, fifth from right) and Yoshiharu Osaka (kneeling, far left).*

Above right photo: *Kanpai after nokai kohaku shiai (end of year training) at ISKF Headquarters.*

Above left photo: *Teruyuki Okazaki (at far left).*

Photo at left: *Teruyuki Okazaki with his secretary, Lois Luzi.*

QUESTION: *The more you advance, looking back to the arts you practiced in your earlier years – Aikido, Judo and Kendo-do — you see the overlapping principles within all Martial Arts or do you think they are all separate entities?*

OKAZAKI: All traditional Martial Arts principles are exactly the same. I have experience with this. I started Kendo in grammar school, and in high school I did a little Judo, and Aikido before Karate. The techniques are a little different of course, just as boxing and wrestling are different, but all of those masters taught the same principle. Budo means never to fight.

The philosophy is also exactly the same --- one movement to defend yourself. I stayed in Karate because I checked all of those body movements and Karate was the best for me. I am lucky; I studied Aikido from Mr. Ueshiba, who was the founder of Aikido. Kendo has many different masters because it was the oldest martial art in Japan, and Judo had many different instructors.

But the way they taught was exactly the same. It has changed now that it has been accepted in the Olympic Games. That is why in Japan a lot of people are not practicing Judo anymore because it is not a real Martial Art now that it is in the Olympics. You can see that not many universities have a Judo club because the students want to study a real Martial Art. It is like wrestling in the U.S.

QUESTION: *Can you please tell us about the significance of the "Seika Tanden" in Budo?*

OKAZAKI: From the time a beginner starts taking classes, I tell them that all power is generated in the seika tanden, which is the area just below the navel. For centuries many Martial Arts instructors believed that there was a spiritual power originating in that area. All techniques originate from the seika tanden and then flow through to the punch or kick. If the body's center or seika tanden is strong, then the technique will be strong also. This would be ki because there is a direct connection between the body's core to the extremities. When energy flows through the center that is ki.

QUESTION: *The Samurai was a man who served, who had no ego, and was always loyal. This is the way of the warrior or Bushido. These of course are principles celebrated the world over. Do you therefore think that the Bushido is not necessarily solely related to Japan but is in fact a universally recognizable set of principles to live by?*

OKAZAKI: I know this is a universal mindset; it's just not called Bushido in countries outside of Japan. Ninety-nine percent of all people feel a loyalty to their government, to their country, and even to their families. This is the same as Bushido. Not all will go to extremes, but most will do what they have to protect what they believe in, whether it is their country's principles or their family's safety.

IN HIS OWN WORDS

Every year ISKF holds a Master Camp with over 60 countries participating. Some of those country's governments do not get along and are always at war. But when these different people come together to train in karate, they are very good friends and respect each other's

Masters Yutaka Yaguchi, Teruyuki Okazaki, Hirokazu Kanazawa and Masaru Miura --- ISKF Master Camp.

cultures. They train together, eat together and sleep together. And I always tell them you now understand the true way of being a martial artist and Budo, this is the mindset you must bring back to your country and this will help to contribute to bring peace to the world. They all say "Osu" because they understand and I know they try the best they can. This is why karate-do must be available for all people worldwide.

It is what Grand Master Funakoshi understood and wanted and I must do my best to continue his mission.

QUESTION: *Sensei, let's talk about some technical aspects of Karate-do. You always mention the importance of good stances. Why is that?*

OKAZAKI: Good karate comes from the bottom --- from your stances. Just like a strong tree can withstand any wind because of its strong foundation, this is the same for karate. For a technique to be strong you must have a strong foundation. Stance training requires focus and dedication. It is boring and I know that but introducing the stance training in the early stages of training will teach the student patience. There is an old saying: "Three years for a horse stance (kiba-dachi)." When you watch a student perform a kata, you can see if the upper body

"leads" the action or if it is the lower body and the stances that "generate" the movement. Stances are very important in karate and actually the solidness of the stances shows the level of the practitioner. The transition from one

Mokuso --- ISKF Master Camp.

stance to the other in kata training is a good way to teach the students how to move the body in a single coordinated, unified motion.

The classic way of stance training where the student stays for 30 or 60 minutes in 'kiba-dachi' is something that you can't do normally these days. It is up to the teacher to find new ways of developing strong stances in a more friendly way.

All instructors should examine their teaching methods and try to develop ways to creatively incorporate the stance training in their programs.

QUESTION: They say the "eyes are the window of the mind." How does eye positioning and sight affect the karateka in kumite and kata training?

OKAZAKI: In kata training always keep your eyes at your own eye level. Do not try to look at your feet or hips to correct yourself. You always keep your eyes at the right level for kata. Do look into the direction of the movement you are doing. Remember kata is "alive" and you are dealing with an opponent so you can't make a movement without "seeing" first where the attack comes from.

In kumite, the eyes show the mental state of the practitioner. You should keep eye contact but don't think that "eye contact" means simply looking. In fact the point where you are looking is not the "main" target of our sight. In many ways, you can "read" your opponent by looking into his eyes. Your can "see" their fear, their doubt, the openings for attack, etc.

Keep your eyes open, don't blink unnecessarily or show a look of weak intentions. Fix your eyes in one place but make your peripheral vision do the work. You have to learn how to develop that peripheral vision in kumite. This is zanshin (to always be focused) whether you are doing kihon, kata and/or kumite.
The eyes focus on the opponent whether they are there or imagined as in kihon and kata, and the zanshin (ready spirit) remains until *yame,* back to natural stance.

QUESTION: *What should be the right attitude in self-defense?*

OKAZAKI: Sometimes self-defense has less to do with the physical aspect and more with the awareness side of it. It is important to develop a certain sense of knowing where the danger is and avoid it. We should try to "foresee" situations where we may be forced to use the fighting techniques we know. I have to emphasize the concept of "Awareness". Don't walk in the streets without being aware of your surroundings, not paying attention to the people next to you, etc. Like "zanshin" after the completion of a technique we should have a constant mental "kamae" to avoid these circumstances.

QUESTION: *What is your advice when you can't avoid that?*

OKAZAKI: Then you have to act to protect your physical integrity or your loved ones. In that extreme situation, I'd recommend to use those techniques that provide a maximum result with the minimum effort. Don't think of a self-defense situation as you think of a "kumite" match in the dojo or in a competition. Self-preservation has nothing to do with these two "controlled" situations. Use more your natural weapons and target those to the weakest areas of your aggressor. If they cut you or hit you do not give up. I always say, if you cut my arm I will take your life. Most importantly, stop your opponent, then get away. It is not necessary to continue the fight.

QUESTION: *Such as?*

OKAZAKI: Use your finger jab, the edge of your hand, your fingers, etc., to attack "soft" areas. The low kick to the aggressor's knee is a good example too. Basically, all the techniques that you would never use in a competition or friendly exchange. It is important to learn the vulnerable

Perfection and focus in every movement.

points. Especially for smaller people to defend against a larger attacker. Know the target areas. And stay aware throughout the exchange!

If you practice your kata seriously and with the idea that you are defending yourself against multiple opponents, then you are continually practicing your self defense. Grand Master Funakoshi always said that if you practice the first 5 Heian's seriously and continually, then you will be practicing the techniques that can defend in any situation.

QUESTION: *What would be your advice to avoid these situations?*

OKAZAKI: Unfortunately, nowadays there are a lot of aggressive people out there. Our society is putting a lot of pressure on individuals and they are under a lot of stress. Some of this stress is self-inflicted too…and it doesn't come from outside but in the end, it is stress.

Try to never put yourself in a dead end situation when you have no choice but to fight.

If you leave ego aside…many of the fights in the street will never happen. Be smart, don't walk up a dark street if you do not have to. From a legal point of view, the karateka must remember that if he does not have a "life threatening" aggression and he attacks another person for a silly ego reason… in a court of law he will have a problem.

Let's not forget that a true karateka never fights with someone of a lower physical level. It is better to walk away than choose the violent way to solve a problem.

QUESTION: *What do you think about Kumite training in the dojo? Should there be contact or non-contact?*

OKAZAKI: It is important to practice everything in the dojo, Kihon, Kata and Kumite with the same thinking. Always serious and always that the one technique you are doing may be the one that you may need to save your life. It doesn't matter big or small, male or female. It is all the same. However, karate is a fighting art and sometimes things happen in the dojo. Everyone must always have a good attitude, you do not want to intentionally hurt someone. But even with the best of intentions, things happen as I said. Remember, keep your courtesy at all times.

QUESTION: *How is Zen related to karate and the Japanese martial arts?*

OKAZAKI: Zen is not martial arts but it was used by old Samurai and Budoka to develop the spiritual and mental state necessary for combat. Samurai had to face death and it was through Zen training that they learned how to control fear and face their own destiny. Our physical actions only are "perfect" in dealing with a threat when the mind does not interfere. That is why Zen is helpful. They accepted death and therefore there was nothing to fear, just do their best. The practitioner of karate can benefit from this training too. It can help us to transcend our ego and become more aware of the Universe. It can teach us to look at things realistically for what they are and not to "resist" unnecessarily. And in combat, to forget about winning or losing and simply "move"!

QUESTION: How difficult is the way of Zen for a student?

OKAZAKI: Philosophers have made a great mistake fostering the idea that Zen is a difficult and inaccessible idea to average people. There is nothing farther from the truth. Zen is around us and in us. It is not something that you learn from books and it is not limited to the martial arts but can extend to all fields of human endeavor. Karate is active Zen, living Zen. This mindset should also be for the karateka when they walk onto the dojo floor, it is scary for everyone, but to keep the Zen spirit and face those fears. This will help the karateka to deal with what comes at them, whether it is another opponent or themselves.

(Continued on Page 149)

Photo at left:
Yoko Geri Kekomi --- none other compares.

Middle left photo:
Teruyuki Okazaki and Carl Shaw demonstrating at ISKF Master Camp.

Middle right photo:
Happy to be at ISKF Master Camp.

Bottom photo:
Teruyuki Okazaki, noted for his flexibility, works at it every day.

TERUYUKI OKAZAKI

Photo at right: *Demonstrating with Masatoshi Nakayama.*

Middle left photo: *Demonstration in the U.S.*

Middle right photo: *Teruyuki Okazaki's Kendo training still visible in his posture.*

Bottom photo: *Masters Teruyuki Okazaki and Yutaka Yaguchi.*

Photo above:
Teruyuki Okazaki opening morning training at ISKF Master Camp. Shigeru Takashina (far left), Yutaka Yaguchi, Stan Schmidt and Masataka Mori.

Photo at right:
Teruyuki Okazaki with former ISKF President Judge Paul Ribner.

Photo at left:
Teruyuki Okazaki at ISKF Master Camp.

Photo at right: *Always a watchful eye on everyone in attendance.*

Photo below: *Professional boxer Joey Giardello challenged Okazaki Sensei in the dojo. Giardello lost!*

Teruyuki Okazaki (below left), and demonstrating a technique with Oded Friedman at ISKF Master Camp (below right).

IN HIS OWN WORDS

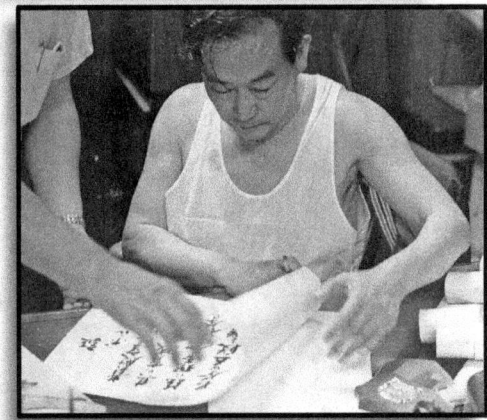

Photo above: *Lois Luzi, Robert Sandler, and Teruyuki Okazaki. Robert Sandler was Okazaki Sensei's longest active student when he came to the U.S.A.*

Photo at right: *Masatoshi Nakayama, a noted caligrapher.*

Photo below left: *Never just giving commands, always sharing full explanations when teaching.*

Photo below right: *In addition to teaching at ISKF Master Camp, Teruyuki Okazaki enjoyed conducting lectures.*

TERUYUKI OKAZAKI

(Continued from Page 143)

QUESTION: *They say karate starts with "respect and courtesy", what exactly does that mean Sensei?*

OKAZAKI: Funakoshi and Nakayama Sensei always emphasized the element of courtesy in karate and in life. Traditionally, a brave man that has no courtesy is disliked by the society. As a martial artist we have courage and strength but the world condemns those who show only those qualities.

Respect and courtesy are extremely important in ancient Japanese thought. Courtesy should be apparent in all our actions and aspect of our life. But by this I don't mean a cold and rigid type of behavior. A true courtesy means a selfless concern about others. I teach this to my students: martial arts begins and ends with courtesy and its rituals must always be performed correctly. That is why we bow to our opponent before and after a match, and also we bow, do seiza, mokoso and bow again to both the instructor in class and to begin and end a competition. This shows courtesy to the teacher for the information they are getting, to their opponent for the lessons learned from them and in a competition for the lessons gained by that experience as well. Everything begins with a bow!

Because of this, it is very important for a karateka to learn how to be courteous. A genuine karateka does not have to show these things and shows respect and courtesy to others. It shows what kind of human being he or she is. He doesn't let his strength to get the better of his judgment!

QUESTION: *Sensei, people talk a lot about the spirituality of karate and martial arts in general. What is your opinion about it?*

OKAZAKI: The spiritual aspect of karate can't be achieved simply by doing some meditation a few days per week. In fact, it is more difficult than the physical side. It is easier to think that it is all about closing your eyes and meditate and say some philosophical words. But that is not it.

To begin with, understanding karate is something experimental and not theoretical. Karate training is the sum of all our experiences; emotional, physical and mental. Once we understand this, we'll start seeing that the separation between these three aspects starts disappearing and all becomes one. It is then when we can start talking about spirituality and begin to communicate with others from heart to heart. Interestingly enough, the more one person is into the spiritual side, the less he or she talks about it. In the book "Tao Te King" which is a Taoist classic, it is written: "Those who know do not speak; those who speak do not know."

The famous Zen scholar, D.T. Suzuki said that "nothing can be said about Zen."

Like I said before, try to communicate with your heart more and less with your head. Remember the Zen master quote: "When meditating, chop off your head, put it by your size and then mediate."

IN HIS OWN WORDS

QUESTION: *From a philosophical and spiritual perspective, what do you think are the biggest differences between the training when you were young and nowadays?*

OKAZAKI: There is a Zen saying: "To gain is suffering, loss is enlightenment." In the old days, the karateka left many things behind in order to practice karate; family, work, friends, money, etc. Today people say: "I want this, I want that". They want fame, medals, trophies, money, material things, etc.

A true karateka looks at their training from the standpoint of loss and not gain. Only when he or she gives up rank, trophies, recognition, fame, popularity, etc.... the practitioner will be close to understand truly the real reason for karate-do training. Karate training and study is training and study about yourself. It has nothing to do with championships, tournaments, ranks, positions and fame. Going back to the Zen master one more time: "To study the self is to forget the self. To forget the self, is to understand all things."

Everything we do in our lives is "karate training". Unfortunately most of practitioners don't see it that way. From washing your hands to cleaning your room, it is all "karate training". But we can not make the mistake of thinking that karate training is a casual thing like washing your hands. Just the opposite! Everything we do must be focused and serious like dojo training. This means constant concentration of body and mind in everything we do!

Your karate training should bring meaning to your life showing who your true self is.

QUESTION: *How can karate training be related to daily life?*

OKAZAKI: Karate training should bring meaning to your life. It should show who your true self is. It teaches how to bring the mind and body together. Nowadays the students seem to forget how karate can be taken into their lives. It does not end when dojo class is finished. It is true that our society has changed and the old "hardcore" mentality has been lost in many ways but nonetheless, the teacher should remind the students that karate is a "way of life".

When the student focuses more on athletic recognition, competitions, tournaments, ranks, diplomas and cash prizes for defeating the opponent, he or she must remember that "those" things have nothing to do with the reality of our lives.

QUESTION: *Sensei, I remember hearing in one of your speeches that "when things are going very good, do not get too happy." Why is that?*

OKAZAKI: In life, everything has a beginning and an end. In nature, the same. A good karateka knows that, because life goes in cycles, his happiness will come to an end. Therefore, he is never too happy about the good times. He or she is cautious and understands the cycle of things.

The same thing applies to when things are going bad. It is harder but we need to learn to control it and accept the fact that if we keep "pushing" and get out of the tunnel, things will be better later on. It takes time to learn this lesson in life but the sooner we do, the better off will be.

QUESTION: *What is your advice for those looking for the right teacher?*

OKAZAKI: Finding the right teacher is probably the most important thing. The problem is that when an individual wants to start training karate, he or she most likely won't know anything about the important elements of the art, so it is very hard to know what to look for. The teacher-student relationship is based on trust. Remember the old samurai traveling long distances to find the right master. When you find a good teacher you should treat him like a treasure.

One time someone contacted our offices and I answered the phone. I explained to the individual several important things about karate philosophy and how we approach the training in our dojo. After a while, he answered that he "loved" what I told him but wondered if we had a training center closer to him because he lived "five miles away from our dojo". I guess it all boils down to how important karate training is for you.

QUESTION: *Sensei, what do you look for when you are giving a dan exam?*

OKAZAKI: You can see a lot about a person when they are taking a test. Just like my instructor Grand Master Funakoshi could see where my mind was during my black belt tests, in addition to checking the form and accuracy of an examinee, I can see where someone's mind is. I look to see if they understand the kata when they are performing it, I check their technique and spirit during kihon and I can see their character when they do kumite. All these things must be checked but also understanding that each person should be doing their personal best based on their circumstances such as age and abilities.

QUESTION: *What are the most important principles of karate or martial arts in general?*

OKAZAKI: That's a difficult question but thinking beyond styles I'd say: make sure your movements are natural. Natural movement at all time. Then a proper and correct posture of your body in any technique you do. Wrong posture will eliminate the maximum effectiveness of any technique. Learn how to relax your body. If you don't relax, the benefits and efficiency will be minimum. And mental concentration. I'd say these probably are, no matter the style you practice, the "basic principles" to be maintained at all times.

IN HIS OWN WORDS

QUESTION: *Teaching today is mainly done for money. How do you feel about it?*

OKAZAKI: There have been questions about if a professional 'sensei' is good or is bad. I am not going to enter into this dilemma but I am going to say this: no matter how prosperous a person is in terms of money, if he has lost sight of the way of karate, he will lack mental tranquility and peace of mind.

QUESTION: *Sensei, you are known for your excellent kicking technique but do you have or ever had a favorite karate technique?*

OKAZAKI: I always liked the kicking aspect of karate but under Funakoshi and Nakayama Sensei, we never were thought of the idea of having "one" favorite technique, per se.
We trained to be good in all the different aspects of the art. But answering your question; it is normal that everybody feel more comfortable with one or two specific techniques and rely more on those than on others. This is not bad but

(Continued on Page 163)

Photo above: *Masatoshi Nakayama (center) giving a lecture, assisted by Teruyuki Okazaki (left) and Hidetaka Nishiyama.*

Above photo: *A young Teruyuki Okazaki demonstrating mae geri.*

Photo at left: *Okazaki practicing a technique with a class.*

Below photo (left to right): *Motokuni Sugiura, Teruyuki Okazaki and Yutaka Yaguchi.*

IN HIS OWN WORDS

Photo at left:
Breathing, concentration and kime

Photo below left:
A young Teruyuki Okazaki.

Photo below right:
Effortless mae geri teaching the use of the supporting leg.

Bottom photo:
ISKF Master Camp.

TERUYUKI OKAZAKI

Photo above: *Teruyuki Okazaki (back row, far right) with Hidetaka Nishiyama to his right;* Photo below: *Assisting Masatoshi Nakayama;* Bottom photo: *Demonstrating Yoko Geri Kekomi with Greer Golden.*

Photo at left:
Assisting Masatoshi Nakayama.

Middle photo:
Hirokazu Kanazawa and Teruyuki Okazaki --- ISKF Master Camp.

Bottom left photo:
Alongside his tree at Camp Green Lane, PA.

Bottom right photo:
Demonstrating attack by multiple opponents with Paul White and Ronald Johnson.

(Continued from Page 158)

I'd advise to dedicate time to these "tokui waza" during your personal training time and never substitute dojo training for your favorite technique training. When we practice at the dojo with seniors and juniors, we must dedicate that time to develop all karate techniques.

Teaching at ISKF Honbu Dojo.

When you train your favorite technique you should do it in a way that it becomes like a reflex to be used under any realistic situation. Only through long hours of training will you develop confidence in that technique. That technique should be effective against any type of opponent. It can be called your "life insurance" if one day you have to protect your life.

IN HIS OWN WORDS

QUESTION: *Nowadays many people use weight training and other forms of strength and conditioning methods to improve their karate. What's you opinion about this?*

OKAZAKI: Let me start saying that karate does not require big muscle to be an effective weapon. Karate training itself will develop the necessary muscle for effective techniques. Of course you can use supplementary training and methods to develop your body in order to be better at karate but if what you want is to be good at karate...train in karate. The effective use of arms and legs is based on using them as extensions of the hara and hips and not because we may have big muscles.

The body of a karateka is different than the body of a judoka or a weight lifter. We train the body to be good at karate, not train in karate to have a good body. A strong body is the by-product of hard karate training and dedication. Today students want to be faster and more powerful. Everything is about the physical.

I'd recommend to stop for a second and think about the training in a more careful way. Let's stand still, think what karate-do means and represents in our lives.

QUESTION: Now with more than sixty years of experience teaching and with all of the countries you have been to, if you could go back in time with all the knowledge you now have would you have done anything differently?

OKAZAKI: I respect each countries culture such as in some countries instead of shaking hands you bow. That kind of thing. But I always tell everyone, no matter what country you are in, in the dojo you have to follow the Japanese culture 100% at the same time respecting each other's culture. Outside the dojo you learn about the other cultures and respect it. It's funny but even at Temple University, some of the students want to continue after the semester and they come here to headquarters to continue their training,

(Continued on Page 170)

IN HIS OWN WORDS

Photo at left:
Assisting Masatoshi Nakayama.

Photo below left:
Yoko Geri Kekomi

Photo below right:
Power even in a stare.

Bottom photo:
Happy to experience the cultures and environments of his travels.

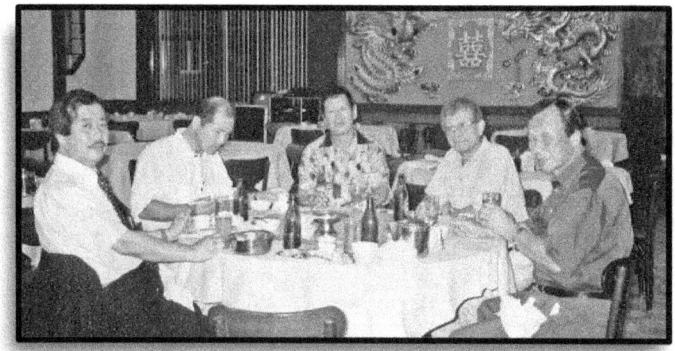

Photo above (left to right): *Hideki Okamoto, Shigeru Takashina, Yutaka Yaguchi, Teruyuki Okazaki and Keinosuke Enoeda;* Photo below left: *Teruyuki Okazaki University Certificate;* Photo below right: *Yoko Geri Kekomi in motion.*

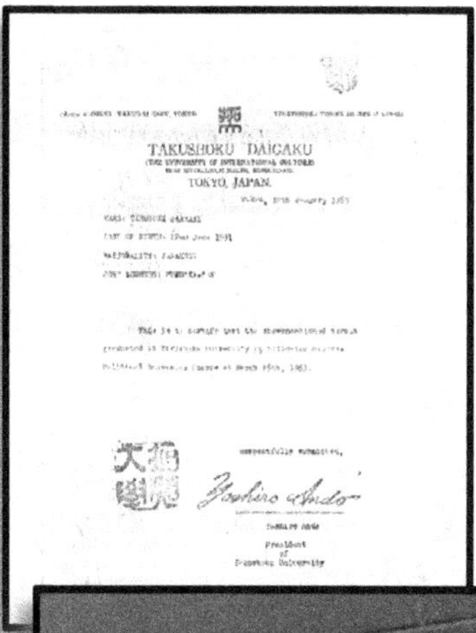

TAKUSHOKU DAIGAKU
TOKYO, JAPAN

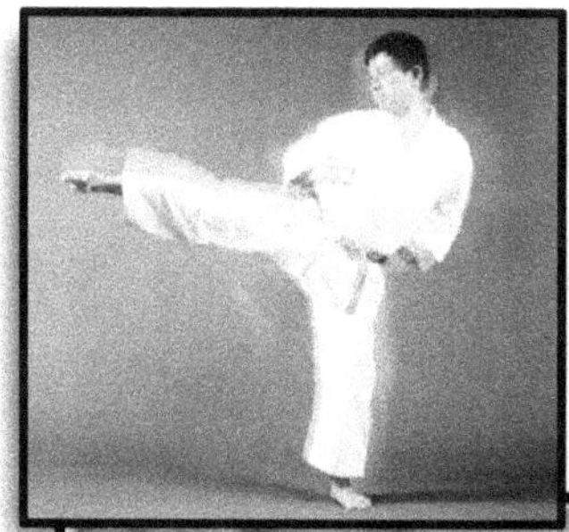

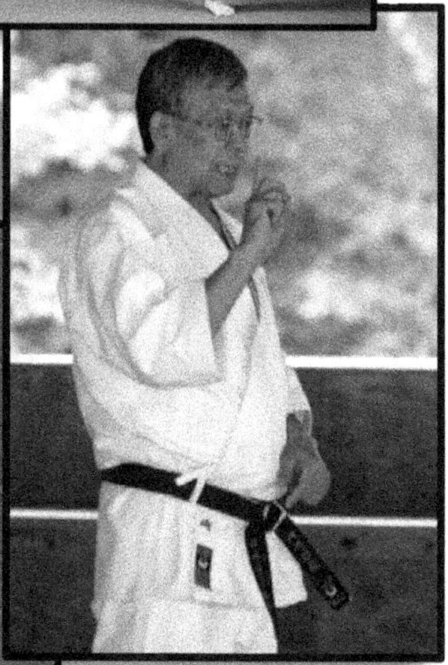

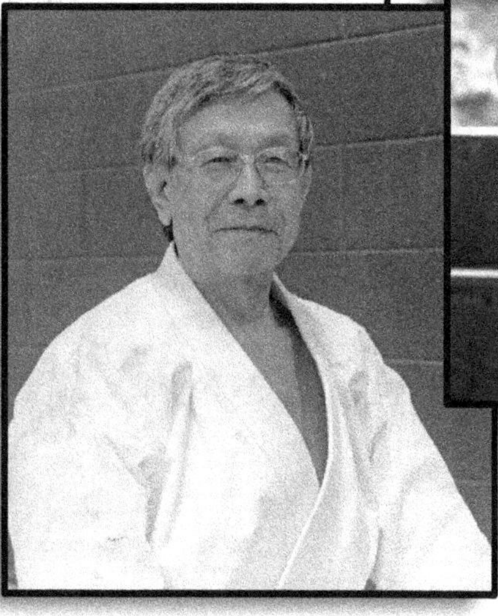

Photo above: *Teruuyuki Okazaki has a way of teaching directly to each and every student.*

Photo at left: *Happy, relaxed and polite.*

Photo at left (from left to right): Shojiro Koyama, Yutaka Yaguchi, Shigeru Takashina, Takayuki Mikami, Teruyuki Okazaki, Stan Schmidt, Masataka Mori and Keinosuke Enoeda --- ISKF Master Camp.

Photo below: *Form and focus.*

Photo below left: *Kamae!* and below right: *Heian Yondan.*

Teruyuki Okazaki (left) training with Hirokazu Kanazawa.

Photo above:
Teruyuki Okazaki and Robert Sandler.

Photo above:
Incomparable posture and form.

Photo at left:
"You say Osu but you don't do it."

Photo above:
Early demonstration.

Photo at left:
Enjoying the class at ISKF Master Camp.

(Continued from Page 158)

and the funny thing is that some of their other professors tell me that the students forget where they are and instead of saying hello to their teachers they bow. But it is still showing respect no matter where they are and they appreciate that. I would not change anything.

QUESTION: *Do you have any regrets?*

OKAZAKI: In retrospect I would say that maybe I could have done some things different but let me tell you this; if you have confidence in your aspirations, words, thoughts and actions and you always do your best, then you won't have regrets of what the outcome is. A brave man is ready to die in the evening if he has understood the truth of the way in the morning. When the death comes, he will be ready to face it with total commitment and composure. The true martial artist is not afraid of death. As Shakespeare's Julius Caesar said: "The coward dies a thousand deaths but the valiant taste of death but once."

QUESTION: *Sensei, how would you like your legacy preserved?*

OKAZAKI: My legacy is the same as my teachers, Grand Master Funakoshi and Master Masatoshi Nakayama – to spread Shotokan karate-do throughout the world, and encourage all karateka to practice not just their techniques, but also to study and practice the Dojo Kun and Shoto Niju Kun. If this is done, then it is my belief that this can contribute to bring peace throughout the world.

QUESTION: *Sensei, how will you pass that on?*

OKAZAKI: I have complete confidence in my nephew Hiroyoshi Okazaki who is more like a son to me that he will carry on this legacy. Not only does he have the form and technique, he also has a good intuition of people and an understanding of sharing the traditional Japanese culture and karate-do to different

societies and countries. He is, after all, of samurai decent. I am very lucky to have him.

QUESTION: *What would you like your last will to be?*

OKAZAKI: I would tell my students the same thing I always have and encourage them to follow Master Funakoshi's philosophy and seek perfection of character, respect others, always endeavor to avoid violent behavior, and be sincere. Those are the final goals we are all aiming for.

QUESTION: *Sensei, people are always asking what is the secret to karate?*

OKAZAKI: It is a lot like making tea.

QUESTION: *How is that?*

OKAZAKI: The secret to making tea is patience. You cannot make good tea just pouring hot water. It must first seep and absorb the leaves to get the full flavor. What was once clear, plain hot water in time becomes wonderful tea. In karate training, you must listen and absorb what you are taught, let it seep in and become you. If you have patience and are open to the knowledge and practice, over time you can become a martial artist. And then you understand what the secret is:

JUST KEEP TRAINING!

ABOUT THE AUTHOR

JOSE M. FRAGUAS is regarded as one of the world's leading authorities and writers in the Martial Arts. With over 45 years of training and after authoring more than 30 books about Karate and Martial Arts, he worked to inspire others to follow, but only a few around the world have successfully brought such drive and scholarship to their work. One of his works, the book series *KARATE MASTERS* – translated into several languages – has become a "classic" around the world and is considered as one of the best all-time sources of information about Karate's philosophy and knowledge.

In addition to his Karate-do training, Fraguas is a Motivational Speaker and Sports "Strength and Conditioning" training specialist. In that area, his focus is on the improvement of athletic capabilities through functional training systems.

IN HIS OWN WORDS

Working both with professional athletes in sports conditioning and non-athletes in more general conditioning, Fraguas has developed unique training programs that integrate proven methods with body-mind-spirit performance enhancement, as well as programs aimed specifically at Martial Arts and Combat Sports performances.

He combines his personal experience, traditional Budo strategies and modern psychology to teach people how to act decisively, using cutting edge skills not only for physical training and sports, but to effectively overcome any challenge in life.

He currently resides in Los Angeles, California.

www.ingramcontent.com/pod-product-compliance
Lightning Source LLC
Chambersburg PA
CBHW052131110526
44591CB00012B/1679